# About the Author

Kenzaburo Oe was born in 1935 on Shikoku island, one of the more isolated and peripheral of Japan's main islands which forms the setting of many of his novels. He left his village for the first time when he was nineteen to study French literature at Tokyo university. Oe published his prize-winning short stories while still a student and his first novel (*Nip the Buds, Shoot the Kids*) in 1958, even before graduation. In 1960 he married Yukari, the sister of the film director Juzo (*Tampopo*) Itami and became a full-time writer, dealing with Japan's post-war situation and the place of young intellectuals.

In 1963 Kenzaburo Oe and his wife had a son who was born with a lesion of the skull through which brain tissue protruded. Unable to decide if they should allow the child to die or agree to an operation which would leave his son permanently brain-damaged, Oe accepted a commission to report on Hiroshima twenty years after the dropping of the atomic bomb. *Hiroshima Notes* chronicles his experiences and reflections over a two-year period. Witnessing Hiroshima and its heroic victims and doctors also convinced him that his son Hikari should be given a chance to live, even if permanently impaired. Hikari, although almost blind and barely able to speak, is now a noted and much acclaimed composer.

Since 1963, a true watershed in his life, Kenzaburo Oe has published about forty novels, books of short stories, critical and political essays and has become one of the world's leading writers whose work perfectly transcends national boundaries. In October 1994 Kenzaburo Oe was awarded the Nobel Prize for Literature.

**Also by Kenzaburo Oe
from Grove Press**

*A Personal Matter*

*Nip the Buds, Shoot the Kids*

*Teach Us to Outgrow Our Madness*

# KENZABURO OE

# HIROSHIMA
# NOTES

Translated by David L. Swain
and Toshi Yonezawa

Grove Press
New York

Originally published in Japan as *Hiroshima Noto* by Iwanami Shoten,
Publishers, Tokyo
First English language edition published in Japan by YMCA Press, Tokyo
This edition first published in the United States and Great Britain in 1995 by
Marion Boyars Publishers

*Published simultaneously in Canada*
*Printed in the United States of America*


Library of Congress Cataloging-in-Publication Data

Ōe, Kenzaburō, 1935–
    [Hiroshimo nōto. English]
    Hiroshima notes / Kenzaburo Oe; translated by David L. Swain and Toshi
Yonezawa.
        p.    cm.
    Previously published: New York: Marion Boyars, 1995.
    ISBN 0-8021-3464-5
    1. Hiroshima-shi (Japan)—History—Bombardment, 1945. 2. Atomic
bomb victims—Japan—Hiroshima-shi. 3. Atomic Bomb—Japan—
Physiological effect. I. Swain, David L., 1927—. II. Yonezawa, Toshi.
III. Title.
    D767.25.H603513    1996
    940.54'25—dc20                                                      96-5812

Grove Press
841 Broadway
New York, NY 10003

00 01 02 03    10 9 8 7 6 5 4 3

# Contents

1995 Introduction   7

Foreword   12

Preface to the English Edition   15

Prologue: Toward Hiroshima   17

ONE  My First Journey to Hiroshima   29

TWO  Hiroshima Revisited   57

THREE  The Moralists of Hiroshima   78

FOUR  On the Dignity of Man   97

FIVE  The Unsurrendered People   114

SIX  An Authentic Man   133

SEVEN  Other Journeys to Hiroshima   149

Epilogue: From Hiroshima   168

Notes   184

**W**ho, in later times, will be able to understand
that we had to fall again into darkness
after we had once known the light?

Sébastien Castilian
*De arte dubitandi* (1562)

# 1995 Introduction

As a child I did not believe the old saying that one's whole life can be decided by the events of a few days. But now, recalling my summertime experiences some thirty-two years ago, I am forced to concede that such a decisive time is surely possible. And I do so with a profound sense of awe.

I was twenty-eight that year, a young novelist who had made a successful debut and was busy building an impressive résumé. Having experienced in boyhood our nation's defeat and then the initial heyday of postwar democracy, I had by that summer of 1963 become a spokesman, through my essays, for the younger generation. Even so, I felt that my career as a writer had already reached a stalemate.

Moreover, in my personal life I faced a real crisis: my first child, a son, had just been born with a severe head abnormality, and would have to undergo emergency surgery. The young doctor, about my age, warned that even if my son's life were saved, he would very likely suffer serious disabilities. So my personal life had clearly reached an impasse.

In these troubled circumstances, I accepted a request to go to Hiroshima that summer to write a report on a large international rally to abolish nuclear weapons — a gathering that, influenced by global trends, was expected to end in serious fragmentation of Japan's peace movement. By the end of my first week in Hiroshima, however, my attitude toward my personal life had been fundamentally changed. The Hiroshima experience also completely altered my literary work. So in a single week a decisive turnabout took place in my life — eschewing all religious connotations, I would still call it a conversion. Today, thirty-two years later, I am even more deeply and surely aware of that determinative shift in my life.

Beginning with that first week, I have since conducted many interviews with survivors of the atomic bombing and with the Hiroshima doctors, themselves survivors, so as to recount their memories, daily lives, and reflections. My essays also depicted the social and political contexts of their lives. But my basic motivation for writing the essays was very personal. Some critics have said that I used bits of Hiroshima's reality as springboards for flights of personal reflection, and in a sense they were right.

Yet today I believe that what I experienced in Hiroshima that summer thirty-two years ago, and the fabric of thought that I personally wove from that experience, contain something distinctly universal. At the very least this experience produced the views of human beings, society, and the world that subsequently shaped my literature. Of this I have been keenly aware during my life and work as a writer ever since that epochal summer. Without that transforming summertime experience, my literary work and my personal life would never have evolved as they did. A few days can indeed determine one's whole life — my experience has led me to believe this 'myth'.

In my Nobel lecture in Stockholm I spoke of things that have evolved from my one-week Hiroshima conversion. I stressed the ambiguities of Japan and the Japanese. But the situation of Hiroshima is even more, and even now, full of ambiguities.

At the time of writing the essays in this book I was sadly lacking in the attitude and ability needed to recast Hiroshima in an Asian perspective. In that respect I reflected the prevailing Japanese outlook on Hiroshima. In response to criticisms from Korea and the Philippines, however, I have since revised my views of Hiroshima. I have focused more on Japan's wars of aggression against Asian peoples, on understanding the atomic bombings of Hiroshima and Nagasaki as one result of those wars, and on the special hardships suffered by the many Koreans who experienced the atomic bombings. These emphases have taken their place alongside the prolonged struggle by Japanese A-bomb survivors for passage of an A-bomb Victims Relief Law.

In the A-bomb survivors' view, Japan's rapid modernization, with its many distortions, led to Japan's wars in Asia, which in turn led to the atomic bombings of Hiroshima and Nagasaki; thus they hold the Japanese state responsible for their sufferings. While they also criticize the United States for dropping the bombs, they have long sought compensation for their suffering from the Japanese government. Last year the A-bomb Victims Relief Law was finally passed, but without any reference to the basic idea of state compensation. This year the national parliament has taken the occasion of the fiftieth postwar anniversary to debate a 'no-war resolution', but this resolution will surely fail to assume full responsibility for Japanese aggression in Asia. Powerful conservative forces will busy themselves in maneuvers to strip it of any such considerations.

For me, the pressing question today is, Did the Japanese really learn anything from the defeat of 1945? In these essays the reader will find that one young writer cried out, three decades ago, for the nation to learn the lessons of Hiroshima. As the record of that urgent call, this book has a vital message for today. I have tried to live by the lessons I learned during my first summer in Hiroshima, and my writing has been based on those lessons. In the concluding paragraphs of my Stockholm lecture, I traced the evolution of my core feelings and thoughts, then expressed a personal hope that had its beginning in the work that produced these essays. It is appropriate therefore to re-state here those concluding thoughts.

In the lecture I recalled that my mentally impaired son Hikari became able to express in music what was not accessible to him in words, and that his earliest efforts were full of fresh splendor and delight. But gradually his music came to express something dark and sorrowful, like the voice of a crying and dark soul. Yet that voice is beautiful, and his ability to express it in music cures him of his dark sorrow in a process of recovery. Moreover, his music has been well received because it heals and restores his contemporary audiences as well. This gives me courage to believe in the wondrous healing power of art.

While I cannot prove this belief, I do rely on it, 'weak person' though I am, to 'suffer dully all the wrongs of Man'* accumulated throughout the twentieth century's monstrous developments in technology. This I do in the hope that, as one with only a peripheral place in the world, I can find decent and humanistic ways to contribute to the healing and reconciliation of all peoples.

KENZABURO OE

DAVID L. SWAIN, Tr.

APRIL 1995

\* W.H. Auden, 'The Novelist'.

# Foreword

This book is a deeply moving statement about the *meaning* of Hiroshima, written as only someone deeply moved himself could write. At the outset (chapter 1), the author gives a clue to the profound impact Hiroshima had on his own life: his first-born child, a son, lay in a hospital incubator with an affliction that would leave the child permanently retarded. While penning these essays on Hiroshima, Oe produced a fictional work (see note 54) in which the main character's first-born has a monstrous deformity; succumbing initially to the temptation to abandon the child to death, the main character in the end commits himself to the child with both hope and forbearance. It is no secret that Oe's own commitment to his afflicted son drew great strength and inspiration from his encounters with the *dignity* of the A-bomb survivors in Hiroshima and with the *authenticity* of those who steadfastly cared for them. The author's rare sensitivity to human extremity, however, is never condescending. Few will easily forget his typically understated depiction of the Hiroshima heroes as 'people who did not commit suicide in spite of everything.'

The translator, Toshi Yonezawa, was born in 1922 in Hokkaido. She studied English literature at Tsuda Juku College in Tokyo, graduating in 1942, and in 1953 completed graduate studies in religion at Tohoku University in Sendai. Since then she has taught English, ethics, and religion at Hirosaki Gakuin College in northern Japan, where she has also served as college chaplain and is currently dean of the general education course. In May 1981 she became an ordained minister of the United Church of Christ in Japan. Her scholarly research and writing have concentrated on Soren Kierkegaard and Paul Tillich. An advisor to the YWCA for twenty-eight years, she is a longtime member of the nationwide Christian Scholars Fellowship. From her rich background and command of the English language, she has produced a thoroughly competent translation; and she very kindly gave me a free hand to make stylistic changes and to ascertain technical details relating to Hiroshima.

Dr Eisei Ishikawa, professor of pathology at Jikei University School of Medicine, who collaborated with me in translating an encyclopedic work on the atomic bombings of Hiroshima and Nagasaki (see explanation to the Notes), kindly checked medical expressions that were brought to his attention. Mr Yasuhiko Yamamoto, assistant to the director of Hiroshima Peace Memorial Hall, gave most generously of his time and expertise to confirm a wide variety of matters relating to Hiroshima and the atomic bombing. Dr James David Reid, former editor of the *Japanese Journal of Religious Studies* and presently professor of the sociology of religion at Tokyo Union Theological Seminary, examined the edited manuscript for clarity and coherence, as did my wife Betty. I am most grateful for so much competent voluntary assistance, though I am responsible for any errors that remain.

The editorial goal was to make the author's own text as directly accessible as possible to the English-language reader. Group and organization names are given in English (and publicly established forms were used when known). Personal names are in the Western order (surname last). Literary and scholarly obtrusions were generally avoided, though Japanese titles of published works (with English equivalents) are provided. Explanatory notes were kept to the minimum, useful for an intelligible reading. Finally, the author's intricate style at times lends itself to both complex and simple English translation; in such instances the translators and editors opted for the more straightforward rendering.

DAVID L. SWAIN

# Preface to the English Edition

This book evolved from the first essay written in 1963 in Hiroshima as an on-the-spot report on the split in the movement against atomic and hydrogen bombs. Despite subsequent attempts to restore unity to the movement, it remains divided, on the political level, to this very day.

Surviving victims of history's first atomic bombing, however, retained unity in their own nationwide body, the Japan Confederation of A-bomb and H-bomb Sufferers Organizations (JCSO); and this body, since its founding in 1956, has continued the movement against nuclear weapons. The JCSO has also persistently urged the government of Japan to enact a law for the relief of A- and H-bomb victims — a law that would provide relief to all such victims as compensation for war damages, not as welfare to individual victims. The distinction is crucial: for, by pressing their case in such terms, the A-bomb victims raise the question of the responsibility of the United States government for dropping the atomic bombs on Hiroshima and Nagasaki, and of the Japanese government for starting the Pacific War. The victims' position also insists that the government of Japan commit itself to working on all international levels for the abolition of nuclear arms. To date the Japanese government has not passed an A-bomb victims relief law; but the victims, though many of them are now elderly, continue to seek passage of such a law.

In its Constitution, Japan has declared to its own people and to the whole world that it renounces war forever. Yet, today, in and around the ruling government party, there are movements afoot to revise the Constitution so as to permit rearmament, which could in time include nuclear arms. The critical moment of decision has arrived, when it will be possible to judge whether the Japanese have emerged from the tragic experience of 'Hiroshima' and 'Nagasaki' to become a new people who truly seek peace. In writing these essays it was my hope — indeed my faith — that the Japanese people who join the A-bomb victims in pressing forward along the difficult and distant road toward eradicating all nuclear weapons will win out over those Japanese who would revamp the Constitution and have our country turn back along the road toward becoming once again a military superpower. If the forces for peace do not win, then it will be clear that we failed to learn the bitter lessons of that tragic experience. And that failure would be a betrayal of those people who somehow maintained their human dignity amidst the most dreadful conditions ever suffered by humankind.

At a time when the nuclear threat to human existence mounts daily, I am most grateful for all who have labored to translate and publish this book in English so that it becomes available to a wider audience of those who share the fervent wish for a world free of nuclear arms.

KENZABURO OE

May 1, 1981

# PROLOGUE
# TOWARD HIROSHIMA
## April 1965

Perhaps it is improper to begin a book with a reference to one's personal experience. But for myself and Mr Ryosuke Yasue, an editor, fellow worker, and companion, all the essays about Hiroshima in this book touch the innermost depths of each of our hearts. Hence, our personal experiences when we first went to Hiroshima in the summer of 1963 are pertinent. For myself, there was no hope of recovery for my first son, who was on the verge of death and lying in an incubator. Mr Yasue had just lost his first daughter. A mutual friend had hung himself in Paris, overwhelmed by the specter of a final world war and of impending nuclear doom — an image that daily flooded his consciousness. We were utterly crushed. Even so, we set out for Hiroshima in midsummer. At no other time have I experienced so exhausting, depressing, and suffocating a journey.

In Hiroshima, the Ninth World Conference against Atomic and Hydrogen Bombs — which would last several days and further deepen our gloom — was beset with much difficulty and bitterness. At first it was doubtful if the conference would be held at all; and when finally convened, it was rent by factions. Swathed with sweat and dust, first sighing and then falling into dark and dreary silence, we merely moved about aimlessly among the crowds of earnest people who had come to the conference.

By the time we were ready to leave Hiroshima a week later, we had found a clue as to how we might extricate ourselves from the deep gloom into which we had fallen. That clue came from the truly human character of the people of Hiroshima.

I was deeply impressed by their genuinely human way of life and thought; indeed, I felt greatly encouraged by them. On the other hand, I felt only pain when I tried to root out the seeds of neurosis and decadence that stemmed from the suffering caused by thoughts of my own son in the incubator. I felt impelled to examine my inner condition and to measure it by the yardstick of Hiroshima and its people. I had received my high school education in the democratic postwar era. In university I had studied language and literature, focusing on modern French literature. When I began to write novels, I was influenced by postwar Japanese and American literature. I had such a short inner history. I simply wanted to reexamine my own thoughts and moral sense — which I assumed I possessed — by looking at them through the eyes of the people of Hiroshima.

After that initial visit, I traveled to Hiroshima several times and recorded my thoughts and impressions in several essays, or 'notes', which were published serially in the monthly journal *Sekai* [World], of which Mr Yasue is the editor. All of the essays are included in this book.

Each time I visited Hiroshima I encountered anew the truly human people of that city. Each encounter filled me with remarkable impressions, though frequently I was saddened by word of the death of friends met previously in Hiroshima. As my essays appeared in *Sekai*, I received a great many earnest letters, particularly from Hiroshima, one of which I wish to quote here. The author of the letter, Mr Yoshitaka Matsusaka, in August 1945 had carried his father on his back so that the father, a doctor, could go to the aid of A-bomb victims. The father himself had been injured in the bombing but worked bravely, like the many courageous doctors I mention in chapter 5. The son bore the wounded doctor to a first-aid station and then throughout the A-bombed city. Today the son is a dermatologist in Hiroshima.

People in Hiroshima prefer to remain silent until they face death. They want to have their own life and death. They do not like to display their misery for use as 'data' in the movement against atomic bombs or in other political struggles. Nor do they like to be regarded as beggars, even though they were in fact victimized by the atomic bomb. Dramatizing their misery to gain relief funds is worse, however, than referring to their suffering in order to oppose nuclear weapons. I agree that we should never be allowed to forget that suffering and misery. But A-bomb victims who have recovered from wounds and regained a normal life prefer to keep their silence. Of course, they would welcome a reduction in taxes as well as a portion of the profits from New Year's greeting card lotteries,[1] but how much effect can beggary and relief campaigns have?

Almost all thinkers and writers have said that it is not good for the A-bomb victims to remain silent; they encourage us to speak out. I detest those who fail to appreciate our feelings about silence. We cannot celebrate August 6; we can only let it pass away with the dead. We are not able to busy ourselves with ostentatious preparations for that day. People who know first-hand the horror of atomic destruction choose to keep silent, or at most speak only a few words and leave their testimony for the historical record. It is only natural, I think, that the antiwar people who spend only one day in Hiroshima on August 6 do not understand the victims' feelings.

This letter came in response to my essay about people who have the right to remain silent about Hiroshima. Although encouraged by the letter, I noted that its harshest criticism was reserved for passages written by me, an outsider to Hiroshima.

Mr Matsusaka also wrote an article for the coterie journal *Haguruma* [Cogwheel], under the pen name Shishio Fukada. In it he put more explicitly the thoughts and feelings expressed in his letter to me, and I discern in his article a fair criticism by a Hiroshima insider toward the outsider. It was, in a word, a voice of self-defense from a young intellectual in Hiroshima. I hope that my own words will be read in connection with his, as quoted below.

The doctors who treated the A-bomb victims, as writer Oe says, could not help being driven to despair when they had to face the continuing after-effects of the bomb that plagued their patients — especially as the doctors were possibly confronted with their own doom. After having issued optimistic reports of no further symptoms of radiation injury, they often had to make bitter corrections in their diagnoses. For my part, however, I was within 1.5 kilometers of the hypocenter at bombing time and suffered only slight exposure symptoms, and am at present in relatively good health. Moreover, my parents, my wife — who at that time was a second-year student in a girls' school and was equally exposed to the bomb — and my three children born in the decade 1955-1965 are all in good health. I therefore tried to be as optimistic as possible, so long as no further ill effects appeared. For this reason I have long wondered why virtually all of the 'A-bomb literature' consists of stories of the miserable people who have not recovered their health, as well as of descriptions of radiation symptoms and the psychology of the A-bomb survivors. Why are there no stories, for example, of families who endured hard times but recovered their health and now live as normal human beings? Must all surviving A-bomb victims eventually meet a tragic death caused by radiation after-effects? Is it not possible for the victims to overcome their illnesses, and their psychological anxiety and inferiority complexes, and thus die a natural death like other people? Must we, instead, all face tragic deaths cursed by radiation after-effects; and must our deaths then be used as data for opposing atomic bombs? Undeniably, our lives were distorted and tormented by the atomic bomb. Yet many other people, though they did not experience the atomic bombings, nonetheless endured the war and knew suffering of varying degrees. Therefore, I determined not to indulge myself in the victim complex that some A-bomb victims in Hiroshima have developed. Although exposed to the atomic bomb, I wanted my body and soul to recover so that I could live my life and die as naturally as people not bombed by nuclear weapons.

Nineteen years after the atomic bombing, my grandmother died a natural death, at age ninety-three, free of A-bomb after-effects. While her life was not altogether happy, she had always enjoyed good health; and she died a natural death without any apparent atomic after-effects. I want to stress that some A-bomb victims do in fact overcome the bomb's effects and die natural deaths. The deaths of A-bomb victims should indeed be properly mourned — but not used only as material for political speeches like those given by outsiders on August 6 in Hiroshima. Thus, I appeal to all to remember that many A-bomb survivors prefer to be ordinary people, to maintain a bright outlook as long as they have no symptoms of A-bomb after-effects, rather than be used as 'data' to oppose atomic bombs.

Mr Matsusaka also wrote in his article the following:

The other day I was shocked to learn that Mr Kikuya Haraguchi, an A-bomb victim and a poet, had hung himself in Nagasaki after being told that he possibly had myeloid leukemia. I learned this from the postscript to his collected poems, published posthumously. I presume that he preferred to die by his own will rather than from a disease caused by the atomic bomb. He wanted his life to end as one, like others, who had nothing to do with the atomic bomb. He sought, that is, to avoid being counted among the A-bomb victims who are grouped together impersonally and inhumanly.

The uneasiness Mr Haraguchi felt about his health could not be clearly explained until a complete diagnosis of A-bomb diseases became available. He simply felt something was wrong, and then was suddenly faced with death. Most A-bomb victims, however, do not have such vague, uncomplicated feelings of uneasiness. They generally suffer clear after-effect symptoms that often foretell sure death. With such a diagnosis, they cannot concern themselves with recovery. They have the terrible burden of learning to live with their illness and of preparing for certain death. I am not sure whether it is better for a doomed A-bomb victim to endure to the end in order to preserve one's human dignity or to end one's life boldly as did Mr Haraguchi and another, Mr Tamiki Hara.

These essays of mine, which have been produced with the direct and indirect cooperation and criticism of Hiroshima people, are now to be published in a single volume with the title *Hiroshima Notes*. But the Hiroshima within me does not come to an end with this publication. On the contrary, I have barely scratched the surface of Hiroshima. The realities of Hiroshima can be forgotten only by those who dare to be deaf, dumb, and blind to them.

In the afternoon of March 22 of this year, a funeral was held for a woman who had committed suicide. She was the widow of Mr Sankichi Toge, who had composed excellent poetry about the misery caused by the atomic bomb and about the dignity of people who refused to surrender to their hardships. There is a rumor that she was crushed by fear of A-bomb-induced cancer. But we should remember that, a few weeks before her suicide, someone had smeared paint on the monument bearing her husband's poem, and this had severely shocked her. The perseverance with which the Hiroshima people bear their miserable solitude is not a dogmatic stoicism. If a cruel person were to take advantage of a crack in the day-to-day effort to persevere, then it would be rather easy, with just a paint brush, to crush the strength of a widow menaced already by the fear of cancer. What else could this widow do but fall into dark depression and keep on sinking — with her memories of her husband who was once exposed to the atomic bomb and had died twelve years ago, losing his strength during a lung operation; and her memories of the monument now stained with hateful, spiteful paint at a time when so many people no longer heed the poet's cry? The parting words of the widow's sister, Nobuko Konishi, a member of the Hiroshima Mothers' Group against Nuclear Weapons, impressed me very much: 'Sister, you performed all things excellently. Your life, like Mr Toge's, left no room for remorse. Thus, I will never hesitate to sing your praises.'

Give back my father, give back my mother;
Give grandpa back, grandma back;
Give me my sons and daughters back.

Give me back myself.
Give back the human race.

As long as this life lasts, this life,
Give back peace
That will never end.

SANKICHI TOGE*

* Source: *Hiroshima Peace Reader*, by Yoshiteru Kosakai, translated by Akira and Michiko Tashiro, and Robert and Alice Ruth Ramseyer. Hiroshima Peace Culture Foundation, 1980. The above English translation, by Miyao Ohara, is carved on the back of the monument dedicated to Sankichi Toge, in the Hiroshima Peace Memorial Park.

This is the cry uttered by the poet for us survivors.. . .

On the same afternoon as Mrs Toge's funeral, a lecture meeting was held in Tokyo to memorialize a writer who had committed suicide in despair and humiliation, crying out for us survivors, for he knew well that the world would take a course contrary to his plea. The writer, Tamiki Hara, who had been exposed to the atomic bomb in Hiroshima, had composed his lucid work, *Natsu no hana* [Flowers of summer], in December 1945 when all the people in Hiroshima were still stunned into silence. In the year following the outbreak of the Korean War, he committed suicide. So long as the memory of such a characteristic Hiroshima person remains, how can the Hiroshima experience ever be brought to an end in anyone's heart?

This spring I journeyed to Okinawa where the people greeted me, a traveler from the main island, with gentle smiles. But among them I met a woman who, try as she might, could not hide her feeling of distrust. She resented having to appear friendly with a frozen smile on her face. I think her attitude was most appropriate. After all, the A-bomb victims in Okinawa have been neglected for twenty years since the war. They returned to their homes in Okinawa after being exposed to the atomic bombs in Hiroshima and Nagasaki; that is, they exiled themselves to remote islands where the doctors did not know how to treat their A-bomb injuries. Subsequent investigations have clearly shown that on the island of Okinawa and the nearby Ishigaki and Miyako islands, many people have died with symptoms of radiation illness. One young man of the Yaeyama Islands, who had been strong enough to become a champion sumo wrestler, was exposed to the atomic bomb at a munitions factory in Nagasaki and afterwards returned to Ishigaki Island. Later, in 1956, he suddenly became paralyzed on one side of his body. Suspecting that he had been affected by radiation, he consulted doctors on his island; but the doctors there naturally knew nothing at all about radiation after-effects, and thus could not treat his illness. Soon he could not move even while sitting, and his body became monstrously swollen. At last, in 1962, this former sumo champion coughed up half a bucketful of blood and died. Even then, there was no doctor in Okinawa who could confirm that his terrible death resulted from radioactive poisoning.

Most of the 135 A-bomb victims listed by the Okinawa Council against Atomic and Hydrogen Bombs feel some degree of physical uneasiness. But all of their complaints have been dismissed by Okinawan doctors as fatigue or neurosis. The blame for this should not be put on the doctors of Okinawa; rather, medical specialists from Japanese hospitals where A-bomb victims have been treated for two decades need to go to Okinawa in order to help the victims there. Can we still be deaf to the needs of angry, helpless A-bomb victims already neglected these many years? Moreover, the Okinawan A-bomb victims with anxious spirits in bodies weakened by the worst monster of this century — the bombs that devastated Hiroshima and Nagasaki — must even now coexist with military bases where nuclear weapons are stored. Yet they have no recourse but to remain silent in the face of this continuing threat to their existence. It is only natural that some of them should drop their smiles and show their distrust and rejection of us. These people are still expecting much of us, though they have already waited patiently for twenty years.

On March 26 the government announced that in April a

medical team will be sent to examine Hiroshima and Nagasaki A-bomb victims living in Okinawa. People who need hospitalization will, through the auspices of the A-bomb Medical Care Council (an advisory body to the Minister of Health and Welfare), be sent to the A-bomb Hospitals in Hiroshima and Nagasaki. Thus, for the first time after twenty years of sheer neglect, a window for Okinawan A-bomb victims has been opened. But it is only a window. I heard of one Okinawan victim who, though encouraged to enter the A-bomb Hospital in Hiroshima, could not make up his mind to do so, for he knew that his family could not manage if he left Okinawa. This may well be the general situation for many in Okinawa. It is well known that Okinawans do not enjoy good medical services. As long as health care in Okinawa remains at its present level, it will be very difficult for A-bomb victims to receive adequate treatment there for radiation injuries, even if medical specialists are sent to Okinawa. I am ashamed that at present I can do no more for them than to record the harsh sentiments of one Okinawan A-bomb victim:

> I wish the Japanese would have more sincerity. They are always afraid of offending the Americans, but they neglect the deeper human problems. If they intend to do anything, they should do it now, in a concrete way. That's what we all want.*

So long as the A-bomb victims' lives and cries are this urgent, who can sweep Hiroshima from his or her consciousness?

* A medical care law for A-bomb victims in Okinawa was enacted in 1966 — a decade after such a law was passed for A-bomb victims on Japan's main islands. Ed.

# CHAPTER ONE:
# MY FIRST JOURNEY TO HIROSHIMA
**August 1963**

As I arrive in Hiroshima in the summer of 1963, day has just dawned. No local citizens have appeared on the streets yet; only travelers stand here and there near the railroad station. On this same morning in the summer of 1945, many travelers had probably just come to Hiroshima. People who had departed from Hiroshima eighteen years ago today or tomorrow would survive; but those who had not left Hiroshima by the day after tomorrow in August 1945 would experience the most merciless human doom of the twentieth century. Some of them would have vanished in an instant, vaporized by the heat and blast of the atomic bomb, while others would live out their cruel destinies, always afraid to have their leukocytes counted?[2]

The morning air is already dry, with a hot white sheen to it. After an hour, the citizens begin to stir. Although it is still early morning, the sun is as bright as it will be at high noon; and it will remain so till evening. Hiroshima no longer looks like a ghost town at dawn; it is now an active city, with the largest number of bars in Japan. Many travelers, including some whites and blacks, mingle among the local citizens. Most of the Japanese travelers are young. The visitors are walking toward the Peace Memorial Park (Heiwa Kinen Koen), bearing flags and singing songs. By the day after tomorrow, over twenty thousand visitors will have come to Hiroshima.

At nine in the morning I am standing in the Hiroshima Peace Memorial Hall, at the main entrance to the Peace Park. After going up and down stairs, and walking back and forth through the corridors, I am finally at a loss about what to do; so I sit down on a bench with other people who, like me, are not sure what is going on. A journalist friend has been coming here for several days and, also uncertain, just sits. The air is full of anxiety: is the Ninth World Conference against Atomic and Hydrogen Bombs[3] really going to be held? Various meetings to prepare for the conference are being held in this Memorial Hall, but almost all are secret meetings. Even though I wear a journalist's badge on my shirt collar, I am shut out of all the meetings. The shut-out journalists and the conference participants who arrived too early ('too early'? — thousands of people are due to arrive in Hiroshima for the Peace March this afternoon, and there is to be a reception for them this evening), and even the regular members of the board of directors of the Japan Council against Atomic and Hydrogen Bombs are all at their wits' end. They slump down on benches, sighing and grumbling 'any country . . .'[4] as if it were a greeting. Initially there was a consensus: 'We oppose nuclear testing done by any country.' But now everyone murmurs 'any country . . .' and sighs gloomily. 'Any country'? What country is meant? The country of the dead? Someone else's country? I recall my first impression of this desolate no-man's land and of the shivering travelers at dawn.

Suddenly everyone jumps up from the benches, and groups roaming the corridors also turn toward one spot. Mr Kaoru Yasui, chairman of the Japan Council against Atomic and Hydrogen Bombs, comes forth to give a progress report on the prolonged secret meeting of the Council's managing directors. If light is at last visible at the end of the tunnel, we mustn't miss it. Since the confusion of last year's conference, Mr Yasui has been useless as chairman of the paralyzed Council. In Shizuoka City, where 'Bikini Day'[5] was held on March 1, the rally theme included the phrase 'any country', again causing such confusion that he tendered his resignation as chairman. I wonder, however, whether the new chairman to be chosen this summer will be able to resolve the issue.

Chairman Yasui enters the room where the regular directors (excluded from the closed session) are waiting. They are now tired, irritated, and somewhat sad; they have waited patiently, utterly ignored, just like the other bench-warmers and corridor-hawks in the Peace Memorial Hall, not to mention all the early arrivals milling about in the shade of trees in the Peace Park. The ignored directors speak to Chairman Yasui in irritated voices mixed with anger and entreaty, or almost a cry. The more outspoken ones ask the chairman and the managing directors in charge of the pending World Conference to explain the delay — and why they, the regular directors, have been ignored so long.

Has the conference been cancelled? asks a director from Kanazawa. Chairman Yasui is neither irritated nor excited. He answers in a powerful and sympathetic tone;

he is sincere and frank, but cautious. 'No, we have not cancelled it. We are in recess. I came here to explain frankly what the managing directors have done.' Empty laughter is heard. Do they laugh because the Kanazawa director is so hysterical, or because the chairman's reply is so stereotyped?

A director from Yokosuka probes further: 'When you spoke to us earlier, didn't you say that if the issues are not settled by the managing directors, you would refer matters to the whole board of directors, including us, to solve them? Don't you acknowledge the authority of the full board of directors?'

Chairman Yasui wards off this question with full sincerity but also avoids its point. 'I have come here to talk frankly.' There are no questions that might drive him into a corner except this one. The directors from Tokyo and Nagano request only that the World Conference be opened. The Tokyo director says, 'More participants than anticipated are now on their way from Tokyo to Hiroshima. Conditions look good for the success of the conference.' But most people feel that the confrontation between the groups mobilized by the Japan Communist Party (JCP) and the Japan Socialist Party (JSP) will have a cancerous effect on the conference.

The excluded directors' voices are pathetically solicitous and void of authority; they might as well have been talking to the moon. Still, the time for the Peace March is only six hours away, and there is no prospect of the conference being ready for the marchers.

Chairman Yasui's tone does not vary. He repeats with passion and sincerity what is clear — perhaps too clear — to any observer. 'There are many complicated differences of opinion among the managing directors.' Then he raises his voice: 'Please give us a little more time.'

He hints that the managing directors are making slow progress. Meanwhile, the regular directors have been totally ignored for a long time. Progress is obstructed by the phrase 'any country' and by differing views of how the conference should deal with the proposed nuclear test-ban treaty. Chairman Yasui uses obtuse and emotional words but never speaks concretely about the obstacles. Differences between the Japan Communist Party, the Japan Socialist Party, the General Council of Trade Unions of Japan (Sohyo), and the foreign delegates to the conference, particularly with regard to the China-Soviet Union confrontation, bring the conference preparations to a standstill. The problems were known to everyone before Chairman Yasui came out to speak; but we hear only the oft-repeated line, 'Give us a little more time.' If the managing directors had plenty of time, would the problems be resolved? No one seems to believe so. At last the chairman goes away without specifying how long 'a little more time' is. The ensuing consultation among the regular directors left behind is fraught with general disagreement and feelings of suspicion. When a suggestion is made, it is immediately trampled underfoot. Some of them begin shouting, and seem ready to fight. They are the ones who had tea with the JSP members. A man who acts as their leader leaves a parting shot: 'You are like people who are separated, or like a divorced couple that lives in the same house.' What does he mean by this? It seems remote from the spirit of consultation.

The Yokosuka director was coarsely denounced by another director; he goes out with me to the balcony, away from the window. As he was told to keep silent in the consultation, this is the only way I can get his opinions. He says, 'The board of directors at its sixtieth session agreed to hold the World Conference despite the divergent opinions. That decision is being ignored here. It is wrong to hold the World Conference while pretending to be in agreement and camouflaging disagreement with deceptive words. The people at the local level are ready to carry on the peace movement without any help from the JCP, the JSP, and Sohyo. The local people are the ones who will promote the movement without losing hope, even if the Japan Council against A- and H-bombs should split.' He is impatient.

Fatigued, the quarreling directors fall silent again. I leave the aborted consultation and walk downstairs. The ground-floor lobby is becoming crowded as participants from various localities arrive to register and pay their conference fees. But with preparations at a standstill, the conference cannot begin. The participants gather in circles, stroll in groups, or practice songs. They are surely as cheerful and untroubled as the Yokosuka director claimed. I sense a real gap between these people and the others — Chairman Yasui, the managing directors in secret session, and the excluded regular directors. The opening ceremony will eventually be held, but how will the gap be bridged? The sun-filled Peace Park is virtually empty. I am moved by the thought that this empty space will soon be filled with twenty thousand people.

Of all the monuments in Hiroshima, the Memorial Cenotaph for the Atomic Bomb Victims[6] is the most frequently visited. I walk toward it. An old woman stands beside it. How often I have seen such people standing still and silently in Hiroshima. On that fateful day in 1945, they saw hell unleashed here. Their eyes are deep, darkened, fearful. 'The Rivers of Hiroshima' (a serial magazine of testimonies, published by the Hiroshima Mothers' Group against Nuclear Weapons) records what two aged women with such eyes saw.

> The sickness was so dreadful, but we could only look on helplessly. My daughter Nanako was so eager to live for the sake of her newborn baby, but she couldn't be saved. And that's not all. After Nanako died, I still had my twenty-six-year-old son Hiromi, and he had keloid scars[7] on his head and hands. Therefore, he couldn't get married, and he tried to commit suicide several times.

Another testimony:

> My two nieces in Toriya township escaped alive but completely naked. Passing one night at Eba,[8] someone gave them a *yukata* [light summer kimono], which they tore into strips and wrapped around their bodies. They looked so miserable that their landlord scorned them as 'infectious'. First the younger one died, then the elder too, saying, 'Auntie, kill me before I become as miserable as she was.' The younger ones all died, leaving me, the old one, all alone.

Suddenly, I recall Mr Kaoru Yasui's passionate but deceptive words, the ready but empty effusion of sincerity that promised nothing concrete: 'Give us a little more time.'

At three in the afternoon I stand in the shade of some

sparse roadside trees in front of the A-bomb Hospital, waiting for the Peace March to come by. Except for reporters, there are only a handful of people along the street and in the space in front of the hospital; they too are waiting to see the marchers. The members of the Hiroshima Council against Atomic and Hydrogen Bombs* cannot leave the Peace Memorial Hall as long as the conference remains stalemated. One of those waiting is the leader of the Hiroshima Mothers' Group against Nuclear Weapons; another is the sponsor of the Hiroshima Ikoi no Ie (Hiroshima Home), a home for orphaned elderly A-bomb victims,[9] the solitary aged who are always haunted by the fear of cancer. These two leaders have worked tirelessly for many years; now they grow impatient. Last night the aged victims of Ikoi no Ie visited countless memorial monuments throughout the city, bearing lanterns, flowers, and incense to console the dead. They were joined by groups from thirty-two city districts. All Hiroshima is one vast graveyard. On every corner in townships throughout the city there are memorial monuments, including some that are no more than a small stone. 'The anti-bomb movement must not become separated from its base among the people of Hiroshima,' the two leaders feel. 'Now that the movement is losing the support of Hiroshima citizens, ordinary people are building a new movement at the local level in this way, walking through the neighborhoods with flowers and incense; and they are welcomed by like-minded people in each place.'

Soon we catch the choral strains of a tape-recorded song, 'We will not tolerate atomic bombs' — played a bit

* The full title is Hiroshima Prefecture Council against Atomic and Hydrogen Bombs; herein the prefectural reference is omitted. Ed.

too slowly — and a hoarse voice over a loudspeaker beckons us to gather. The Peace March is approaching. The A-bomb Hospital windows are filled with attentive faces; some patients come out on the porch-like roof over the entrance. The young woman patients no longer wear shredded *yukata*; now they have on colorful summer robes. This may be the only real change in their lives since the war, for the deep anxiety remains in their hearts.

The marchers clearly suffer from fatigue and the heat; their pinched faces remind me of insects. But their eyes are shining. The faces of those who have marched the full distance are terribly sunburned. The march comes to a halt before the hospital, and the marchers crowd into its front yard. Attention focuses on some marchers, bare-shouldered like Buddhist priests, who have marched at both Auschwitz and Hiroshima. The nose and cheeks of a blond woman from West Germany are fiery red, painfully burned by the bright sun. The hospital yard is now completely jammed.

From the hospital entrance, three patients emerge into the glaring sunlight. One is a lovely teen-aged girl, her head swathed with bandages. She smiles brightly as she straightens the skirt of her rose-colored, flower-patterned robe when the breeze blows it away. Following brief words of greeting, flowers are presented to the patients. Representing the patients, a small middle-aged man begins to make a speech in a mosquito-like voice, holding his head high and erect like an Awa doll. He ignores the hot pavement and speaks fervently, but is interrupted by a loudspeaker announcing the departure of the marchers. I can barely hear his last words: 'I believe the Ninth World Conference will be a success.'

Holding the bouquet of flowers and dropping his shoulders in resignation (the heat, after all, is too much for an A-bomb patient), he withdraws with obvious satisfaction and dignity. It is an impressive scene. If a patient were to cast a stone at the marchers, out of irritation with the delay in conference preparations, the Council against A- and H-bombs could hardly protest. The patients, however, are waving innocently and with great expectations, as though the marchers were their only hope. There is something awesomely inspiring about it all. Even if the marchers are greeted only by the politically poisoned secret meetings when they cross the large Peace Bridge to reach the Peace Park, the march itself will have been purified and given significance by the patients' expectant faces and welcoming gestures.

I walk with the marchers in the sunshine. Except for a very few, the citizens of Hiroshima are quite cold toward the Peace March, yet very alert to reported difficulties in the preparations; they seem to sense what will materialize after the march, and watch the proceedings with curiosity. As the marchers stop for a rest just short of the Peace Bridge, a bit of news reaches them; it has just been decided that the World Conference will be officially sponsored not by the national Japan Council against A- and H-bombs but by the local Hiroshima Council against A- and H-bombs. The Peace March soon regains its vitality and enters the Peace Park, swelling to several times its initial size as others join. The park's earlier sun-baked emptiness is now filled with the bustle and excitement of World Conference Eve activity. The marchers proceed through the gathered crowd, greeted by cheers and applause. A propaganda truck of the Japan Communist Party leads the welcome, but no one voices any opposition to it. Is the political pendulum swinging toward support of the JCP?[10] At the moment, nothing is clear. The JCP, JSP, and Sohyo continue their fierce competition to mobilize followers.

Sunset gives a rose tint to the spaces between the bomb-bent steel frames of the A-bomb Dome.[11] The opening in the Memorial Cenotaph, which resembles a large Haniwa clay figure, already grows dim. It is five in the afternoon. On the platform in front of the cenotaph stand the leaders of various groups — Mr Yasui and the secret session participants, the foreign delegates, and some of the sunburnt marchers. The gathered crowd sits on the grass, facing the platform. Mr Ichiro Moritaki, representative director of the Hiroshima Council against A- and H-bombs, approaches the microphone with obvious tenseness. He is also a leader of the national organization of A-bomb victims.[12] The tension manifested by this old philosopher is somewhat like that of the patient who spoke in a small voice in front of the A-bomb Hospital. The health of the old philosopher, himself an A-bomb victim, is in a precarious condition. He announces: 'The Japan Council against Atomic and Hydrogen Bombs has entrusted complete management of the World Conference to the Hiroshima Council against Atomic and Hydrogen Bombs.' Applause rises and fades away into the beautiful evening sky. But the applause does not match that given another statement made by a priest who had marched at Auschwitz: 'Hiroshima is hotter than Africa.' The next speech draws even greater applause. Mr Yasui comes to the microphone, leans forward slightly, and waves his hands in cadence with his voice as he exclaims pathetically that he has just transferred to the Hiroshima Council against A- and H-bombs all the problems which his own Japan Council could not resolve. He cries that the Hiroshima and Japan councils had decided to open the World Conference jointly, thirty minutes before the Peace March reached the Peace Park — as if the timing were an important factor. 'Action, more than argument, will make the peace movement a success!' The crowd applauds vigorously.

I am shocked. Chairman Yasui had asked for more time when he spoke to the regular directors earlier and then ignored them. That time was for discussing, thinking, and resolving problems. But under pressure, just thirty minutes before the Peace March arrived, the managing directors quit trying to resolve issues and simply passed through the crisis with their eyes closed. 'Action, more than argument. . . ,' he says. Does this mean that the unresolved stalemate is merely hoisted onto the local Hiroshima Council? That emotional phrase, 'action more than argument. . . ,' continues to evoke great applause. I have often seen such an emotional appeal elicit a similar emotional response from a crowd — and this crowd today includes active members of the peace movement from districts throughout Japan. The appeal is 'action more than argument,' but the dispute does not thereby recede quietly into the shadows at this World Conference; it emerges forcefully into the light from the moment the conference opens.

Mr Aung-bak Chen from China derides the nuclear test-ban treaty as deceitful; if America really wants peace, he says, it should remove its military bases from Japan. A black youth from Cameroon, wearing a black-and-white striped jacket and a wine-colored hat, also denounces the nuclear test-ban treaty; he shouts, '*Uhuru* [peace], *uhuru, uhuru,*' in his own language. A woman delegate from the Soviet Union proceeds to the microphone and asserts, 'It would be a great step forward, as Mr Khrushchev has said, to sign the treaty tomorrow.' Her statement, too, evokes considerable applause, though people of the host country openly ignore it. It seems but one act in the overall drama of this conference — the scenario of which may well have been rehearsed in the closed preparatory sessions. But none of the participants, after all, knows what part these theoretical theatrics will play in the eventual outcome of the conference. I am impressed by the sight of the pale face of philosopher Moritaki (the Hiroshima representative) in the growing dimness of twilight.

At half past nine in the evening, I stand among people looking through a balcony window at the managing directors' meeting. They are now joined by the regular directors, ignored during the day, who must decide whether to approve the delegating of power to the Hiroshima Council. The managing directors had earlier voted 14 in favor, 11 against that decision. Through the window we watch the present vote tallied: 49 in favor, 7 against, 11 reservations, and 3 abstentions. The opposing votes are cast by directors aligned with the peace committee. Later the same night, at another place, the Hiroshima Council formally accepts the decision.

Hiroshima at night is hot. After their meeting, the perspiring directors come out on the balcony which faces the darkness over the river and the Peace Bridge. The minority's irritation is clearly visible even in the dark. They seem to have premonitions, and anxiety, that the decision essentially solves nothing, and that great confusion will follow and further aggravate difficulties. The Kanazawa director had wanted to urge the managing directors to apologize for shifting the problem to the Hiroshima Council at the last moment, but he could not get the floor to press his proposal. The director from Yamaguchi says that the problem is to prevent further meddling by the managing directors; the need is to create a new style of peace movement centered in Hiroshima. He looks gloomy, and not just because he is tired. Necessarily worried about the future of the conference, the minority generally feels that the Hiroshima Council could function better if the managing directors would criticize their own inability to conduct the conference and explain fully why they passed responsibility to the local council. The Hiroshima Council people, in any case, have had a bad situation suddenly dumped upon them and will get no sleep until dawn. Despite difficulties and misgivings, they must get busy. The hottest rumor among people close to the Peace Memorial Hall tonight is that the Yoyogi faction (the Japan Communist Party) will withdraw from the conference proceedings. This rumor keeps cropping up.

There are many people in Hiroshima tonight who must work on without a wink of sleep. The doctors at the A-bomb Hospital are doing their best to save a young girl; but she will die, and their sleepless efforts will have been in vain.


Now it is morning. Ten o'clock. I am climbing up Hijiyama hill to the institute where the deceased girl's corpse was taken last night. The place is as bright, clean, and functional as a mirror. The institution is the Atomic Bomb Casualty Commission (ABCC), founded to study atomic bomb diseases, including causes of death. Nowadays they also offer some treatment to A-bomb victims; but the people of Hiroshima do not like to come up here, so cars from the ABCC motor pool must fetch them. Picking up patients and bringing in corpses are, they say, the two most unpleasant jobs at the ABCC. In the waiting area of the lobby, a few patients sit calmly. One is a child waiting while its mother receives a medical examination; another is a young girl, herself a patient. All are very quiet, patiently awaiting their turns. Another car from the motor pool departs for the city; the drivers work as hard as anyone at the ABCC. This is one of the two places on earth where the effects of atomic bombs on human beings are investigated in detail (and who of the twentieth century can be uninterested in what they learn here?).

I look into various rooms near where the corpse of the young girl who died yesterday lies waiting for an autopsy to be performed. In one room, two women laboratory technicians are examining blood smears stained by Wright's method; they are recording the number of leukocytes on hand calculators. Under the microscope, the dyed leukocytes look like grapes. I peep at a glass slide on which there is a blood smear containing 90,000 leukocytes per cubic millimeter. A woman doctor in charge of this room says that she once met an old man with a 830,000-leukocyte count in his blood. Needless to say, the old man is dead now. The person whose blood I am presently looking at is already dead, too. This bright modern place itself is the land of the dead. 'Do you know,' I am asked, 'how many leukocytes a healthy person has?' Confused for a moment, I figure, 'If a deathly sick man had 830,000, then a normal person must have. . . .' I am told that I have only 6,000. I quickly lose interest in looking through the microscope. In the next room, tissues imbedded in paraffin are being cut into thin sections. For the first time I can relax in a room where an A-bomb victim's blood is examined for syphilis. Never again will syphilis seem so simple and harmless to me as it did this morning.

Looking for a way out, I walk down a corridor next to the data room where thousands of clinical charts are filed. An IBM machine is collating the identification cards of patients, and the moving cards, making a sound like running water, can be heard through the closed door. The card of the old man who had 830,000 leukocytes, cancer in all his internal organs, and a backbone that became like pumice, may be one of the cards. I cannot help shivering. Leaving the ABCC and going down into the streets of Hiroshima, I realize that no one up on the hilltop referred to the World Conference against Atomic and Hydrogen Bombs. In fact, no one even mentioned it. It is as though the conference were an event taking place in some faraway city.

At eleven in the morning, a small fracas develops at the information desk for conference participants, upstairs in the Peace Memorial Hall. Someone is protesting that the number of representatives admitted is fewer than requested. Is this one more sign of the fierce competition among the Japan Communist Party, the Japan Socialist Party, and the General Council of Trade Unions? People working for the Hiroshima Council say, however, that this is only one of the many problems encountered during the morning. The man persists in his protest; but in general, the preparations are going smoothly. The World Conference will be held. At least, everyone now thinks so; and in that mood they are getting ready for it. People working directly for the conference and participants from the local districts are going about their tasks very efficiently.

As I leave the Peace Park, I buy a copy of the *Akahata* ['Red Flag' news organ of the Japan Communist Party] and learn for the first time that the JCP has decided to reject totally the limited nuclear test-ban treaty — just when the treaty is being signed in Moscow. Each time I get near the Peace Park, I smell the strong odor of politics. It requires considerable patience to find a taxi in the bustle between the Peace Park and Peace Bridge. While I am waiting, conference participants pour into the park. Will they all be admitted as representatives? Rumor has it that all hotels in Hiroshima are full. Today the population of the city has swelled by twenty percent.

I go over to Hiroshima Red Cross Hospital and sit face to face with its director, Dr Fumio Shigeto, who is also the director of the A-bomb Hospital. He had arrived in Hiroshima to take up his new post just a week before the day of the bombing in August 1945. He was exposed to the bomb and injured while standing in line waiting for a streetcar. It was a light injury; and, in any case, he could not rest as a patient. In the open space in front of his hospital, thousands of dead bodies had to be piled up each day and then cremated in its yard. He had to stay on duty, directing the wounded doctors and nurses engaged in caring for dying people. Moreover, the hospital itself had sustained heavy damages. Dr Shigeto is a large, big-hearted man of action with simple, peasant-like features and a deep, frank voice. He must have worked in an amazing way during those first postbombing days, yet he also found time to study perceptively the yet unknown effects of the atomic bomb. What little time could be snatched from his hospital duties he devoted to investigations, visiting the bombed area by bicycle to collect burnt stones and tiles. These specimens are now displayed in a room of the hospital. Compared with the IBM-collated data at the ABCC, his data are sparse, indeed. But Dr Shigeto collected his materials with his own hands and resources. One aged A-bomb victim, in an impressive act of cooperation, contributed all his completely affected bones as specimens. It so happens that Dr Shigeto had been interested in radiology in his younger years, long before the atomic bomb was dropped on Hiroshima, and thus had a sense of direction in his solitary research. He discovered, for instance, that hermetically sealed X-ray films stored in the hospital cellar were exposed by the atomic bomb.[13] He was one of the first Japanese to recognize on his own the nature of the atomic bomb on the bombing day.

From that day to this he has continued his research while devoting himself also to sustained treatment of patients. He draws on his experience, the hospital records, and clinical observations to determine the nature of A-bomb diseases and to fight them. Initially, he thought that A-bomb illnesses could be cured within a few years — until he found that leukemia was among the illnesses. Certainly the atomic assault was the worst disaster to befall mankind, and there is no way to know how radiation affects human bodies apart from clinical work and the discoveries made in actual clinical situations. It took seven years of sustained, painstaking research before a firm statistical connection between radiation and leukemia could be made. Subsequently, he reached a statistical conclusion that the incidence of leukemia was decreasing; but the hope generated was later betrayed, as the statistical curve rose again. How many other such human impressions, based on persistent trial and error, will turn out similarly? Along with research, Dr Shigeto has had to undertake political efforts to reform the general health care system and build up his hospital. In his own mind, judging from actual contact with patients, the connection between radiation and cancer is clear; but it is difficult to get the Ministry of Health and Welfare to acknowledge the link. As if all this were not enough, as director of the hospital he must also deal with the difficulty that A-bomb victims have in finding marital partners.

Dr Shigeto takes me to visit some of the patients. One is an old man with rough, dry, darkened skin, peeling in flakes that resemble shreds of twisted paper. He lies limply and greets the doctor in a hoarse voice. He seems annoyed because he tried to smile easily but could not do so. When, suddenly, I think that this old man might have tried to wave to yesterday's peace marchers, it wrenches my heart. The doctor himself has been filled with bitter grief at parting with patients more seriously ill than this old man — old people with cancer or leukemia, for example, who could do nothing but despair. Even so, such elderly patients must have waved to the peace marchers yesterday. If so, how could the marchers have avoided feeling that they were taking advantage of such old people? At the corner of the corridor stands an old woman who, surprised and breathing heavily, greets the doctor with sobbing. She is weeping for joy, for she just walked ten meters for the first time since entering the hospital. 'Oh, sir, I'm so happy!' She speaks brokenly, through tears. I shall never forget Dr Shigeto's gloomy but gentle look, his eyes like an ox's, upon hearing her greeting. If leukemia attacks, a patient may live six months or a year. Medical therapy can give temporary respite, but not for long. When the leukocytes increase, it is fatal. The doctor questions present uses of chemotherapy for the unsolved riddle of leukemia; for, though the leukocyte increase can be arrested, it eventually returns to a fatal rate. The deep sorrow and anxiety in Dr Shigeto's eyes as he chats with leukemia patients is unforgettable. The doctor himself is an A-bomb victim; he, too, witnessed that hell. He is a typical Hiroshima man who keeps up the fight against the A-bomb after-effects that even now remain deep in human bodies.

At a quarter past seven in the evening, the pale twilight that precedes moonrise silhouettes like dark waves the participants who have completely filled the Peace Park lawn. They include representatives from districts throughout Japan. The mood is tense, for the opening of the World Conference has not yet been formally announced. The platform chairs in front of the Memorial Cenotaph are all vacant. This is because about sixty students of the National Federation of Students Self-governing Associations (Zengakuren) have occupied the space between the platform and the gathered representatives, and are shouting for attention and trying to make speeches. The official conference loudspeaker is warning the students to withdraw and warning the representatives not to be provoked into using force by the students' taunts. The students sing the 'Internationale'. Atop a small truck parked at the center of the student group, the National Federation leader is reading an appeal 'to all workers, students, and citizens participating in the Ninth World Conference against Atomic and Hydrogen Bombs.' (The Ninth World Conference itself makes a strong appeal against war and for peace among all people; but it has been in trouble throughout preparations, and decided by majority vote to turn everything over to the Hiroshima Council. So, what was decided? Was any clear direction given to the struggle against war and for peace?) Behind the students, a group of Buddhist priests are praying, while beating small hand drums. Helicopters are circling overhead, and rocket-like fireworks are streaking up and exploding. The conference participants are trying to drown out the students' song with loud calls of 'peace, peace.' The Peace Park is filled with an air of violent tension and tumult. A right-wing propaganda car is cruising around the park, blaring a military march. A roped-off area in the Peace Park is reserved for the conference representatives and reporters. Local citizens gather outside the ropes and watch silently.

At twenty-five past seven, several hundred policemen emerge from the open space beneath the Peace Museum and enter the park; they head straight for the Memorial Cenotaph, as if to pay homage to the dead. Applause erupts; the conference representatives sitting on the grass are clapping their hands. The disharmony of this scene shocks me. All of a sudden, the students are quickly hauled off. At a point about one hundred meters from the platform, the students are pushed out of the park by the policemen. Voices cry out, and confusion reigns. Someone among the seated representatives calls out, 'Don't let the students intrude!' He shoves away some students who are running from the policemen. The students are soon put to rout; some run toward the reporters on the platform. Some reporters, including myself, are thrown into confusion. I drop down on my knees, and am bruised. A student dashes behind me like a rugby player streaking toward the goal; he cuts toward the rope marker, falls suddenly, and is caught by the policemen. I wonder if one of the representatives tripped him; the representatives, after all, are furious with the students. Why so? One student escapes the police and disappears over the rope markers into the crowd of citizens, shouting back, 'The Communist Party opens a conference guarded by policemen!' It is whispered about that it was Communist members of the Diet who called in the police.

As soon as the students are gone, the Communist members of the Diet are the first to mount the platform. The representatives welcome them with stormy applause. They are followed by the foreign delegates. By 7.50 pm, all the platform chairs are filled. Mr Mitsuru Ito, General Secretary of the Hiroshima Council against A- and H-bombs, proceeds to the microphone to make some opening remarks. 'We are not entirely satisfied with the way the conference has been opened. So, we have decided to return management of the conference to the Japan Council against A- and H-bombs if and when our conditions are met.' Applause is followed by a moment of silent prayer. At eight o'clock, a full moon rises, softly illuminating the twisted frames of the A-bomb Dome behind General Secretary Ito and the local representative, philosopher Moritaki, as they bow their heads silently. These two must shoulder the heaviest responsibilities on behalf of the twenty thousand people gathered here.

Representative Moritaki, of the Hiroshima Council, opens his report with words of remembrance for the dead and the surviving A-bomb victims. Adhering to the Hiroshima experience, the old philosopher's rationale firmly links the hearts and minds of the Hiroshima A-bomb victims to the humanism of the wider movement against nuclear weapons. As he addresses the conference in front of the Memorial Cenotaph, another and quite different activity takes place behind him (in front of the cenotaph). Families of the dead are offering flowers and burning incense. They seem not to have noticed the crowd in the park nor heard the shouts and applause. To me they seem to be playing the part of the chorus in a Greek tragedy, adding dignity to the agony and ecstasy of the drama on the conference platform. Philosopher Moritaki, steadily supported by the chorus from behind, continues to speak to the twenty thousand people.

Gradually, the conference representatives begin to relax. They are no longer interested in the report being given by Moritaki. Some are even booing and hooting at it — which shows that the old philosopher bravely refuses to ignore the most controversial issues. He refers to the phrase 'any country...', and speaks in favor of the nuclear test-ban treaty. This prompts antagonistic noises but only moderate applause. When he refers to the Polaris submarine and the F-105D fighter plane,[14] thunderous applause fills the park for the first time. I sense anew the immense human energy brought to this memorial place by such a midsummer gathering of twenty thousand people from districts all over Japan. I respect the work they do in their local areas and the passion they bring to the anti-nuclear movement. But I am dismayed at the obvious gap between the twenty thousand and the old philosopher who represents both the Hiroshima Council and the national organization of A-bomb victims. The gap widens even as he reads his report.

Already tired, director Moritaki summons all his flagging strength to conclude with an emphasis on unity and solidarity. The applause is sparse and brief. The old philosopher does not yet know that the General Council of Trade Unions (Sohyo) and the Japan Socialist Party have deserted the conference — though he soon will know and feel that he has been betrayed. And when the conference ends, his report having been thoroughly rejected, and when he and the Hiroshima Council find themselves in the worst kind of situation (mocking Chairman Ito's promise, '. . . if and when our conditions are met'), he will again feel betrayed.

After the Ninth World Conference is over, some will assess its outcome as successful and hopeful; others will feel it ended in disappointment and failure. The majority will find themselves between these two extremes. But all will surely realize that the key to the conference's outcome was in the opening ceremony.

One of them is an elderly woman in Hiroshima, herself an A-bomb victim and an active worker in the peace movement (as well as the wife of philosopher Moritaki). In a logical and concrete way, with charm and dignity, she gave me the following account of events on the opening night, including what the old philosopher did after he left the crowd.

Some people from the police station came to see my husband and explained that Communist members of the Diet had asked the police to expel from the Peace Park all persons without an official representative's identifying badge. This action may have been taken in order to gain unity; but the local citizens were shocked to see the representatives making way for the police officers, crying out, 'Here come the policemen,' and then cheering them on. It is sometimes difficult to appreciate and accept the students' way of doing things; but the mutual hostility among the conference people is just as intolerable. My husband came home dead tired and went to bed, saying only, 'Mr Ito and I will participate no more [in the conference].' My husband is not a manipulator or a calculating person; he has simply devoted himself to the anti-nuclear movement and to the association of A-bomb victims because he is a philosopher and thinks that to do so is the moral imperative of our time. But he is physically and mentally exhausted; and once he regains his strength, he would, I think, like to start a new peace movement. Avoiding a nuclear war is important, but we must first abolish all nuclear weapons. The nuclear arms race itself makes people very anxious; and to overcome that, we must oppose all nuclear weapons, mustn't we?

Mayor Shinzo Hamai of Hiroshima also speaks of a new peace movement. He, too, experienced the August 1945 hell and, like Dr Shigeto and the Moritakis, is a true Hiroshima person who has devoted himself to working for peace. 'Whatever course is taken hereafter, there can be no peace movement that disregards the original spirit of Hiroshima. I think it is time to break off all relations with the Japan Council against A- and H-bombs and to begin a new peace movement.'

It is now six in the morning, August 6. Surviving families of
the A-bomb dead are coming to lay flowers before the
Memorial Cenotaph. Soon there is a large floral mound;
and incense smoke wafts up slowly like a mist. The chant-
ing of a united Buddhist memorial service at the A-bomb
Memorial Mound is heard, and the crowd of citizens
increases gradually. A newspaper with the headlineWORLD
CONFERENCE FINALLY SPLITS is blowing in the breeze. The
citizens congregating in the Peace Park are dressed up as
if for a festive occasion. At a quarter past eight, doves
released near the Memorial Cenotaph take wing; and
gathered citizens, now almost filling the park, bow in silent
prayer. A helicopter and a small plane circle overhead.
During the time of silent prayer, the shrilling of cicadas is
heard; but their sound is soon lost in the renewed bustle of
the crowd. The cicadas will be heard no more today, for
the crowd's activity will go on till midnight.

Many meetings are planned in Hiroshima today. Since
last night's opening ceremony, however, I sense that my
interest in Hiroshima has changed. I feel that I am an
unknown traveler who just happens to be at these political
gatherings. But once I get out of the meetings, I am able to
see Hiroshima afresh; and I try to perceive things as deeply
and clearly as I can. This is the first trip on which I feel that
I have encountered the real Hiroshima; and I sense that I
will be coming back many times to work at gaining an
understanding of the true Hiroshima people. My sudden
awakening and new grasp of the Hiroshima experience
has come, for example, from joining a meeting of A-bomb
victims, lasting until midnight, in the Kodo Kaikan, an
assembly hall in Dobashi township. The proceedings were
marked by carefully expressed questions and answers, by

carefully considered appeals and understandings. Their interest was focused especially on the problems of proper medical care for the A-bomb victims dispersed throughout the nation. (Doctors in other cities do not have the same awareness of A-bomb illnesses as do the doctors in Hiroshima; this difference makes it difficult for victims in other places to obtain the A-bomb health books, issued by the Ministry of Health and Welfare, that would make them eligible for medical care at government expense.[15]) For instance, a young couple, both of whom experienced the atomic bombing of Hiroshima but married after they had each left the bombed city, had a child who sometimes becomes anemic. They brought their child to Hiroshima because doctors in their city are not familiar with treatment of A-bomb related symptoms.

On my last night in Hiroshima, I go out to watch the Buddhist service of floating lanterns on the river to honor the dead. I attend to honor my friend who committed suicide in Paris from hysterical fear of nuclear war. The red, white, and sometimes blue lanterns, set afloat near the Peace Bridge, flow upstream as high tide comes in. In the postwar years this custom has found a place in the hearts of Hiroshima's citizens as though it had been a folk tradition for centuries. Countless lanterns drift soundlessly, illuminating the rivers of Hiroshima.[16]

As I leave Hiroshima by plane the following morning, I see the rivers of Hiroshima gleaming in the morning light. A special correspondent of the *Times* of London confides that he had difficulty understanding the import of the noisy catcalls of 'peace, peace' at the conference's closing ceremony held in the packed Hiroshima Prefectural Gymnasium. Japan Council chairman Yasui had said, 'Action,

more than argument. . . .' But were the conference representatives ever given a chance to take any rational and
specific action other than the catcalling of 'peace, peace'?
The leaders held secret meetings to balance things among
the political parties and the various foreign delegations;
the followers merely called out 'peace, peace,' however
energetically. If all that Chairman Yasui could do was to
link these activities by his emotional eloquence, what is to
become of the Japanese peace movement? Such was the
concern of the young Englishman, and I share his concern. The two of us fall silent and look down at the seven
rivers under a sea of clouds.

Then, suddenly, I feel a compelling urge to speak to him
about Dr Shigeto, Mr and Mrs Moritaki, Mayor Hamai,
and other true Hiroshima people, including the patients
at the A-bomb Hospital. This urge stems from my deeper
determination to return repeatedly in order to discover
the true Hiroshima through these people who impressed
me so deeply. I begin to speak to the English correspondent. At the very time that the conference closed with shouts
of 'peace, peace,' the betrayed old philosopher, at another
place, had spoken with keen appreciation of 'the remarkable energy of the people participating in the movement.'
Then he had expressed his own hope: 'In this fateful place,
Hiroshima, the movement against atomic and hydrogen
bombs will be reborn, like a phoenix, and begin anew to
develop into a truly nationwide movement.'

# CHAPTER TWO:
# HIROSHIMA REVISITED
**August 1964**

As our airplane circles over Hiroshima on this day in
August 1964, making its approach to the airport that juts
out into the bay on the city's south side, the seven rivers of
Hiroshima suddenly lose their natural color and glisten
like polished metal. Passengers looking down from their
windows are dazzled by the reflected midsummer sunlight
and withdraw their gaze from the too strong glare. I recall
a similar dazzling sheen on the rivers a year ago when I left
Hiroshima. My sense of time blurs; the departure and the
return, though one year apart, seem to be a continuous
sequence of sightseeing. If Hiroshima viewed from aloft
seems unchanged, so it is with the city seen from a taxi after
we land. The cabbie is excited about last night's baseball
game; it was the same with the driver who took me to the
airport a year ago.

Important changes, however, have occurred during the
past twelve months. Forty-seven patients at the A-bomb
Hospital have died. Most of them were older patients —
sixty-five, sixty-four, fifty-five. The oldest was a woman of

eighty-two who died of cancer of the liver. In fact, most of the deaths were due to cancer. I remember that there were three old men lying abed in the same ward at the A-bomb Hospital last summer. Their skin was dry and rough, and very dark. Something like the crumbs from a rubber eraser protruded from all over their skin. They were solitary old men with no place to go even if they recovered and could leave the hospital. Some of them may already be dead.

According to statistics, the recent dead also include young people. During the winter just past, a young mother in her late teens died of acute myeloid leukemia. She had been exposed to the atomic bomb when she was a new-born baby; after eighteen years she developed symptoms of leukemia and died soon after giving birth to her own baby. Her newborn child thus far shows no sign of abnormality; and that — if the word 'hope' may be used in this case — is the infant's only hope.

I have heard many other miserable accounts of young A-bomb victim mothers who died soon after childbirth, both in and out of hospitals. Such mothers have a heavy double anxiety: that their babies may be abnormal, and that they themselves may die of an A-bomb disease soon after delivery. Even so, this girl in her late teens fell in love, married, and had a baby. I think such courage in the face of desperate anxiety may be called truly human; it shows both human weakness and human strength. I pray that this mother's new baby will grow up healthy as a sign of true hope.

Last summer I met another young mother who entered the A-bomb Hospital when she noticed something strange about her health for the first time following childbirth. Fortunately she escaped danger because she received proper medical care right away. But after being discharged from the hospital last autumn, she had to return early this summer. Her baby is healthy, and this gives her hope. Again, I pray that she will get well soon, and that all young mothers in such circumstances will recover.

Among this year's dead was Mr Sadao Miyamoto, who passed away cherishing a pathetic wish. A year ago, three patients of the A-bomb Hospital stepped slowly into the hot sunshine to greet the peace marchers. At the center of these three stood a middle-aged patient with a very pale face and holding his head erect. He was a small man, shorter than the girl standing beside him in her rose-colored, flower-patterned robe. 'I believe the Ninth World Conference will be a success,' he had said in his strained small voice with a somewhat militaristic tone. Accepting a bouquet and dropping his shoulders, he had then withdrawn into the hospital lobby.

That was the last time I saw him. He had withdrawn toward his death, bouquet in hand and shoulders drooping limply, but with evident satisfaction and dignity. The day after he had entered the place where we outsiders are not permitted to go, he could not stand by his own strength. He spent his last days lying in bed, from late summer through autumn, and then died at the onset of winter. On his hospital chart it is written that he died of general prostration. Dr Shigeto relates, in a sad and faltering voice, how he became so frail, like so many A-bomb patients who suddenly take a turn for the worse and then die. This scholar-physician, who has seen many A-bomb patients waste away due to general prostration, could only say that A-bomb after-effects seem to erode the human body's powers of resistance to illness.

When this small, middle-aged man braved the heat at

high noon a year ago to affirm his hope in the World
Conference, he very likely shortened his own life. The
sacrifice was made willingly, to convey his sincere wish —
though it was interrupted by the loudspeaker of the Peace
March's lead car, and thus could hardly have reached the
marcher's ears — and then he withdrew with satisfaction
and dignity. But the Ninth World Conference, which had
opened that very evening, can hardly be said to have been
successful. Certainly its outcome was far from what the
bed-ridden A-bomb patient had wished; perhaps the patient's hope was quickened by impatience, with death so
near at hand. In any case, the prospect of a total ban on
nuclear weapons was dim, indeed, and progress on a
limited test-ban — which had stirred hopeful sensations in
the A-bomb Hospital patients — had become doubtful
during the Ninth World Conference. At such a time, death
overtook him.

Perhaps this small, zealous patient, at risk to his own
already endangered life, had chosen to contribute to the
anti-nuclear movement by speaking a few encouraging
words; and thus he possibly hoped to cast away fear of his
impending death and the anxiety that his life would end
meaninglessly on a hospital bed. But when death finally
took him, the darkness that nuclear weapons cast over the
world remained as before. Did he lose all hope for himself,
overwhelmed by fear and anxiety, the moment he awak-
ened from his 'vision' of the peace movement's potential?
If not, then at least he must have met his lonely death with
deep regret. And that cannot be redeemed, not even by
the thousands of conference participants who will fill
Hiroshima for the next few days.

Shortly before his death, Mr Miyamoto indicated his

desire to leave the hospital and collected all his savings and belongings. Did this not suggest that he had lost faith in the peace marchers and conference-goers and simply wanted to go home, a man whose trust was betrayed?

> I would be comforted
> if all living things
> in heaven and earth
> were to perish
> in utter desolation.

TAKEO TAKAHASHI

No doubt there are peace movement participants who can reply in sufficiently critical terms to this A-bomb victim's poem. But those who witnessed all of the summer 1963 events in Hiroshima will know that there is no adequate response to Mr Miyamoto, who greeted the peace marchers in his mosquito-like voice and then died when winter came. Among the A-bomb Hospital patients, he was called the last man who maintained a strong interest in the peace movement and in the negotiations for a nuclear test-ban treaty.

This year the Peace March again visited the A-bomb Hospital. The march was led by the Socialist Party. And, again, the patients viewed the marchers from the windows and veranda-like roof over the entrance. Patients with only light injuries sat in a row in the shade of the hospital. The patients all looked older than they did last summer, and the colors of their robes appeared faded and plain. Although I waited anxiously, no patients came out to greet the marchers. It was not because the hospital, considering last summer's example, prohibited them from doing so. Rather, no patient could be found this time who wanted to express his wish for the success of the peace movement. That is why Mr Miyamoto was called 'the last man'.

The few short sentences he left behind begin as follows: 'I appeal from Hiroshima, where mankind experienced the atomic bomb for the first time, for even today many people are suffering from leukemia, anemia, and liver disorders; and they are struggling toward a miserable death.'

All who read these sentences should understand that the phrase 'struggling toward a miserable death' does not mean that they are struggling to attain new life in the face of, or against, a miserable death; it means, rather, that they must struggle along the way to, and until they meet, a miserable death. His words continue: 'But I am really afraid of my future. In this hospital [the A-bomb Hospital], some people have committed suicide or become insane when they learned that their illness had been diagnosed as an A-bomb disease.'

His sentences end with a somewhat futile solicitation, though some people may not agree that it is futile. It is, however, the impression his words leave me with. 'Lastly, I plead that all of you will cooperate to bring about a bright, warless world.'

Early last winter he died, and a too bright summer has come again to Hiroshima. Besides reports on war in Laos and Vietnam, the newspapers tell about three conferences against atomic and hydrogen bombs being held in Japan.[17] Forty-seven people met miserable, unredeemable deaths between the two summers — last summer, and now another not all that different. The bed-ridden patients in the A-bomb Hospital continue to persevere, tormented with anxiety. On the streets of Hiroshima I meet here and there those who share with me their memories of people who passed away during the past one year. But conversation is often cut off abruptly; we each mop our perspiring faces and glance over at Hijiyama hill — in common recognition that eventually there will be no one left here in Hiroshima to keep the memories of the dead as fully as do the data cards in the computers of the ABCC on top of that hill. The cards record in detail the diseased bones, the cancers in all parts of the human body, the awesome numbers of leukocytes, and so on.

I go over to the Labor Hall near the downtown business section. The main meeting place of last year's conference was the Peace Memorial Hall in the Peace Park. There the doors had been closed on secret sessions filled with anxiety. Everyone had wondered if the Ninth World Conference would be held at all, and the corridors had been alive with whispered difficulties and conflicts over the phrase 'any country'.

In the Labor Hall where one of this year's conferences is meeting, there is no such secrecy, anxiety, difficulty, or conflict. If the rather amateurish management of the conference causes some misunderstanding or congestion, no one is upset. Everyone believes that the Three-Prefecture Liaison Conference being held here (with another session in Nagasaki) will proceed smoothly.

Then I look in on the International Conference.[18] Last year, this forum was the hottest battlefield. I recall the heated dispute between Mr Tzu-ch'i Chu, the Chinese delegate, and Mr Georgij A. Zhukov, the Soviet delegate, and the hostile camps mobilized around these two. This year Mr Zhukov is again in Hiroshima as the Soviet delegate. A generous-looking Slavic man who moves his large frame about briskly, his face is always beaming; his obvious self-confidence suggests that he feels himself to be the most important participant in the International Conference, which does in fact proceed in harmony with his mood. A woman delegate from India (who, to me, has the appearance of a corn doll) fully supports the nuclear test-ban treaty, while an equally charming woman delegate from West Germany explains moves in her country to go nuclear and proposes a concrete protest against France's nuclear testing. She, particularly, is calm, concise, and persuasive. 'Let us prevent France and China from conducting nuclear tests, and go on to accomplish complete disarmament. No more Hiroshimas,' she urges, and wins applause. The poison of the Sino-Soviet antagonism which wasted so much energy and produced so many dry and barren speeches at last year's conference, does not appear to have retained the power to spoil this one, too.

While this conference focuses on the nuclear test-ban treaty, my mind inevitably turns to yet another conference being held at the same time in a different place — the Tenth World Conference against Atomic and Hydrogen Bombs,[19] in Kyoto. There the Chinese delegate must be all Oriental smiles, confident that he must lead the Kyoto conference as generously and shrewdly as Mr Zhukov does the International Conference in Hiroshima. And, of course, many meaningful speeches may be made.

The smiling mood of these two foreign delegates will quickly cool and stiffen if they chance to meet again. The more harmonious the two conferences become in separate settings, the more deeply rooted will be the opposition between the two smiling leaders and their respective positions. Mr Zhukov had already experienced a rejection so cool as to freeze his smiles at an international gathering sponsored by the Japan Council against A- and H-bombs in a Tokyo hotel before he came to Hiroshima.

Yet, here comes another smile to be followed by applause. The delegate from Colombia makes a speech, and the conference is all the more serene and harmonious. The haze of smiles is too thick to permit clear perception of either the danger of the anti-nuclear movement splitting further or the buds of reunion that lurk in the background. Before the present split can be overcome, the two hostile camps must first undergo a process in which their smiles turn into sour scowls and their sweet words become venomous ones. Only thus can the seriousness of the schism and the hopeless difficulty of reunion that stem from this International Conference in Hiroshima be thoroughly and genuinely probed. In the smooth proceedings and friendly mood of the present conference, I sense a kind of futility (it resembles the hollow feeling we have when we hear of a mountaineering party making progress by avoiding the most difficult route). This feeling does not disappear when I witness the opening assembly attended by twenty thousand young people.

Professor Moritaki, the old philosopher, mounts the platform and is welcomed with a response no less enthusiastic than that given the Sohyo and Socialist Party leaders at the opening assembly. He is the man who, last year, spoke of his hope, only to be crudely betrayed in the rupture of the Japan Council against A- and H-bombs. During the year since then, he has been working for that hope; and he is one of the most morally influential persons in the shaping of this year's conference. Professor Moritaki knows well that it takes organizations like the Socialist Party and the General Council of Trade Unions to put together a conference of this size; yet he must experience a moment of discomfort as he stands there on the platform. At present it is impossible to develop a large-scale peace movement without a strong organizational base, but some crucial problems elude even powerful organizations. There are those, then, who try to deal with these crucial problems in moral terms; and I find it most inspiring that those who do so are among the true Hiroshima people. Indeed, it is to discover such people that I have come again to Hiroshima.

It was such people who, at the conference of scholars and other intellectuals, [20] first proposed the compilation of a 'white paper' on atomic and hydrogen bomb damages. This conference went smoothly at first, but things changed when Mr Toshihiro Kanai, an editorial writer for the *Chugoku Shinbun* [regional newspaper published in Hiroshima], began to explain the white paper proposal. In the various meetings of this year's summer conference in Hiroshima, Mr Kanai is the only Japanese who is really indignant and excited (he has the bearing of a sober-minded, lower-ranking samurai at the time of the Meiji Restoration of 1868). He once responded to a careless comment of a young journalist by saying, 'Ordinary people also get angry and have difficulty in expressing their anger. We also experience that difficulty.' He said this in broken speech, almost in tears. There may have been observers who felt his excitement was unwarranted but it stemmed from the indignation that had built up in him over nineteen years. For ten years[21] after the atomic bomb was dropped there was so little public discussion of the bomb or of radioactivity that even the *Chugoku Shinburn*, the major newspaper of the city where the atomic bomb was dropped, did not have the movable type for 'atomic bomb' or 'radioactivity'. The silence continued so long because the U.S. Army Surgeons Investigation Team in the fall of 1945 had issued a mistaken statement: all people expected to die from the radiation effects of the atomic bomb had by then already died; accordingly, no further cases of physiological effects due to residual radiation would be acknowledged. As a newspaperman, he had endured the long silence.

Now the time had come for the Hiroshima people to speak out, but was the voice concrete and effective enough? Each summer Mr Kanai must have placed great expectations in the world conferences, and as often he must have been bitterly disappointed. (This is not to malign the *Chugoku Shinbun*; anyone who spends a summer in Hiroshima knows that this newspaper gives the most thorough coverage of the atomic bomb and of movements against it, as well as the most reliable reporting of A-bomb memorial events.) After such long endurance and so much discouragement, the plan for a white paper on A-bomb victims and the damages they have suffered was for him a proposal not to be ignored or rejected. For one who had really cared for the victims so long, the indignation was not inappropriate.

Mr Kanai presses the question: 'Is the atomic bomb known better for its immense power or for the human misery it causes?' He emphasizes that Hiroshima and Nagasaki are clearly known throughout the world because the power of the atomic bomb was demonstrated there, not because of the suffering of the A-bomb victims.

In order to make the Three-Prefecture Liaison Conference in Hiroshima the starting point for a nationwide mass movement, going beyond the limited peace movement of the Socialist Party, the General Council of Trade Unions, and the pro-Soviet groups, we must pay more attention to the essential task of seeing that the basic experiences of Hiroshima, Nagasaki, and Yaizu[22] become well known all over the world. It is stressed that the hydrogen bomb is far more powerful than the earlier Hiroshima-type atomic bomb; hence, the nations of the world tend to ignore or forget the great human misery caused by the 'smaller' bomb. Disputations focus on specifying the enemies of peace, and the elementary effort to inform the world about the original experience of being bombed with atomic weapons is thus neglected. The fervent desire of the A-bomb victims now is, on behalf of all the dead and all survivors, to make sure that the peoples of the world fully understand the nature and extent of human misery, not just the destructive capacity, of an atomic bombing.

The white paper on A-bomb victims and damages is intended to make just such an appeal to the world. For editorial writer Kanai, the white paper task includes 'a survey of the A-bomb victims' unresolved problems and the formation of policies for the health maintenance and relief of the victims.' His phrase 'unresolved problems' has wide implications. For example, the real situation of people who left Hiroshima and Nagasaki after exposure to the atomic bomb is hardly known.[23] Little is known about the

A-bomb victims in Okinawa, who desperately need medical attention from specialists on Japan's main island, nor about the health and livelihood of approximately four thousand victims now living in Tokyo.[24] Each of us is uninformed about A-bomb victims in our own neighborhoods. 'Positive action to survey the actual conditions of the A-bomb victims in our cities, towns, and neighborhoods, so that they may get the medical examinations and relief they need,' is precisely the goal of the movement to compile a white paper. And the 'neglected grievances' to be heard include those of secondary victims of radiation who entered the two bombed cities soon after the atomic bombings; they are not eligible for free medical examinations, as provided under the A-bomb Victims Medical Care Law (1957), unless 'they are already ill and dying.' For an A-bomb disease to be that advanced means to face certain death. It is most important, as Dr Shigeto urges, that exposed victims be checked for any blood abnormalities as early as possible if the lives of the A-bomb victims are to be saved.[25]

Mr Kanai frankly acknowledges that he carefully considered which of this year's three conferences to choose for the presentation of his white paper proposal. His caution and decision are suggestive. Most participants of this [Three-Prefecture Liaison] conference show their belief in their own orthodoxy by ignoring the Kyoto conference;[26] they are quite content and without misgivings within the framework of their own conference. But he challenges them: 'If any of you are not altogether satisfied and have any doubts, then you may want to discuss matters with any of the Kyoto conference who have similar doubts and misgivings. Such would be the most direct way toward reunion.' No signs, however, have appeared that this is likely to happen; the participants of each conference are too convinced of the propriety of their own views. Mr Kanai was much freer in assessing the three conferences and in selecting one for presenting his proposal. His career as a journalist throughout the ten years of silence and the next nine years of open discussion left him less than fully trusted by this conference involving ordinary people. But he overcame the distrust to bring his concrete proposal before the gathered participants; the proposal's concreteness lay precisely in its frank criticism of the schism in the peace movement. In a larger sense, it can be said to be a criticism of all Japanese national movements. The Japanese people's attitudes, after all, are most affected by a person whose lifework is in direct touch with the actuality of Hiroshima. Such is the uniqueness of this 'place of destiny', Hiroshima.

Mr Kanai concludes his explanation of the white paper proposal as follows:

> Clearly the government of Japan is controlled by the conservative party; but, just as clearly, the government does not exist solely for the conservative party. Let us try, therefore, to win both conservative and progressive support in the Diet for a law that affords adequate relief to the A-bomb victims; and for that purpose, we must persuade the government of Japan — the first and only country to suffer atomic bombings — to prepare a white paper on the A-bomb victims and damage, and to make its contents known around the world through the agencies of the United Nations. In the pursuit of these goals lies hidden the potential for a nationwide peace movement, for an undivided peace movement.

The need to compile a white paper and to appeal to the world are extensions of the need to provide adequate relief to the A-bomb victims and other war victims. Next year is the twentieth anniversary of the atomic bombings. For a peace movement rooted in the experiences of those victimized by atomic bombs, it seems to me most fitting, and in accord with the participants' true intentions, that a conference meeting in Hiroshima this summer should give birth to a proposal to compile an accurate and objective document on the real situation of the A-bomb victims, and that it should take steps to disseminate that information internationally.

This proposal is, to my way of thinking, the most forward-looking of all opinions voiced at the conference and it comes closest to expressing the essence of the twentieth anniversary, in 1965, of the atomic bombings.

The A-bomb victims held their own consultation, at which I heard yet another testimony concerning the ten years of silence and the following nine years of open discussion. The victim who gave the testimony was an old man who had lost one eye. As a matter of fact, Professor Moritaki also lost his sight in one eye nineteen years ago at a work place where, as a teacher of Hiroshima Higher Normal School, he was mobilized with his students. He still has his old ink-stained diary of those days. On that fateful day of the bombing, he was at his desk and had just written an account of the previous day (August 5, 1945). 'A beautiful sunrise. Made 500 bamboo spears.' The next moment, the atomic bomb exploded, and he lost the sight of one eye, as did some of his students. Due to that fierce flash of intense light, there must have been a great many people who lost their eyesight.

The old man's greeting to the A-bomb victims' consultation was impressive. Not a conventional greeting, it was, rather, a rundown of the history of movements by A-bomb victims against atomic bombs. At the First World Conference against Atomic and Hydrogen Bombs, the victims had their first opportunity, after ten years of silence, to make themselves heard in a national-scale forum. But at that conference, a prudent group opposed having the victims speak, cautioning that public exposure would embarrass them. But were they really ashamed to air their feelings in public? 'I am very fortunate to still be alive now!' This widely publicized statement was made by an ordinary A-bomb victim who was given a chance to speak at that time — a chance that helped him find meaning in his frustrated life. Does this not clearly suggest what life was like for him during the silent years? Back during the Korean War, the United Press bureau chief in Tokyo came to see a friend of this old man. The friend had lost his sight entirely. Referring to the war in Korea, which at the time happened to be at a standstill, the U.P. bureau chief asked the blind A-bomb victim, 'I suppose we could end the war if we dropped two or three atomic bombs on Korea; as an A-bomb victim, what's your opinion?'

Such insensitivity is already a kind of corruption. And if this corruption should reach an extreme, the final world war, one using nuclear weapons, could easily break out. One function of the national movement against nuclear arms is to issue a warning against this sort of base corruption, and this function has been performed quite effectively. At least today there are no journalists who dare to say to a blind A-bomb victim, 'We could end the war in Vietnam if we dropped a nuclear bomb or two; what do you think?'

On the earlier occasion, the blind A-bomb victim had answered the U.P. bureau chief, 'Sure, you could probably end the war with two or three atomic bombs, and make America the dominant power in the world. But, then, no one would ever trust America.' The old blind victim had countered with the wisdom of one powerless person in Hiroshima where, under occupation restrictions, people had to keep silent; and a few years later he passed away quietly.

At the close of his greeting to the A-bomb victims' consultation, the one-eyed victim related an episode in which, yesterday, people returning from the Kyoto conference had entered the Peace Park, holding flowers, and people of the three-prefecture conference had greeted them with applause. Somehow, the rupture in the anti-nuclear movement may yet be healed. . . .

I did not personally witness that scene, and thus do not know how pregnant it may have been with the seeds of reunion. But no one can doubt that it moved this particular A-bomb victim to express his sincere wish for unity in the anti-nuclear movement.

Certainly the Peace Park is peaceful and quiet this year; there is no evident atmosphere of dissension and dispute. As I sit on the park grass on the memorial day, waiting for the ceremony to begin, I feel a tranquility not only in the overcast sky and over the distant grayish-blue mountains, but also throughout the city they encompass. There was no such tranquility to be felt here on the same day and hour last year. (In the afternoon of this nineteenth memorial day, there are occasional showers — something so rare during the past nineteen years that people remark on it as though it were a mysterious happening.)

Following greetings at the A-bomb victims' consultation, questions and answers are exchanged. The whole atmosphere is earnest and sincere; though the content of the exchange, I notice, is the same as last year's. The young people who have come from all over Japan are concerned, but they are not well-informed about A-bomb diseases or about the A-bomb victims' lives. So, the victim who just finished giving the opening greeting must patiently repeat the same basic explanations that he gave a year ago — and may have to repeat for several years to come. I cannot help thinking again how many truly patient people there are in Hiroshima. They are astonishingly patient.. . .

One of the most patient of them all, Dr Shigeto, is forever coping with a multitude of questions about everything from medical to political matters, as I recall he did last summer at the A-bomb Hospital. He had to deal with forty-seven deaths between the two summers. The National Diet has at last begun to take an interest in a law for the relief of A-bomb victims. Hence, he has had to receive inquiry groups of both conservatives and progressives. A Diet member may, for instance, observe an old bed-ridden patient and ask, 'Why is rheumatism related to the A-bomb?' How is the doctor to reply? If any hospital in the world can answer such a question, it is this one. Do the Diet members fail to understand that *no* symptom can be excluded from a possible relation to the atomic bomb, given the enormity and complexity — far from fully understood — of the damages experienced. Nonetheless, Dr Shigeto spares no pains in trying to explain sincerely, as he busily moves his seemingly stolid but really energetic body about the hospital. When the Russian delegate this summer indicated the Soviet Union's interest in sending medical equipment, Dr Shigeto went right away to see the delegate and settle the matter tactfully. He is careful to steer clear of the superficial swirl of political maneuvering, but never misses any opportunity to improve the capability of the A-bomb Hospital or to enhance concretely the welfare of the patients. In that sense, he sometimes refers to himself as a 'dirty handkerchief.' That is, he serves to filter political purposes out of relief efforts so that the effect on patients is purely and concretely humane.

Dr Shigeto hopes, for example, to develop ways to help the young women who, because of their cruelly disfigured faces,[27] are so ashamed that they have confined themselves to the back rooms of their homes for nineteen years. 'Conscientious doctors' may make responsible examinations and conclude that the young women, for their own protection, should refrain from engaging in social activities outside the home. In Hiroshima, more than a thousand people with disfigured faces stay confined to their homes without adequate attention and protection. In Dr Shigeto's realistic judgment, a reliable program of medical care may enable many of these people to come out of seclusion and become socially active again.

The pressing problem that Dr Shigeto faces this summer, as a medical scholar, is blood abnormality in children whose parents have died of A-bomb (radiation) diseases. Coping with the brave late-teen mother who died after delivery, and with the forty-seven others who died since last summer, brings Dr Shigeto and his colleagues one step nearer to some solution. The 'problem of the next generation of A-bomb patients' (the haunting question of genetics) is one that neither the doctors nor the patients are eager to confront.

Despite the understandable taboo on the question of possible genetic effects, he is convinced that all children of A-bomb victims should be given medical examinations, and that the children should therefore be included in the protection provided by the A-bomb Victims Medical Care Law. His basic premise is that help needed by A-bomb victims and their families should be guaranteed by the state through legal means. During the 'religious war of the peace movement' (to use Mr Kanai's phrase), it was the conservative government that managed to push through a policy to provide funds and facilities for aid to A-bomb victims, and it is conservative Diet members who are now working to extend the scope of such aid. I have often heard of the indecent conduct of a certain local conservative politician in Hiroshima during and after the war; yet, objectively considered, it cannot be denied that he was one of the influential persons in political negotiations to promote aid to A-bomb victims. In such times we feel all the more acutely the necessity of having a man such as Dr Shigeto who works steadily to carry out aid policies responsibly, a man who is convinced that the investment made will ultimately reap dividends for all mankind. Throughout the nineteen years since medical treatment for injuries heretofore unknown became necessary, Dr Shigeto has consistently insisted that the doctors involved in the care of A-bomb patients reexamine the data repeatedly and meet regularly to discuss possible ways of improving both therapy and procedures.

The current plan to review comprehensively the history of medical treatment of A-bomb diseases, scheduled for completion by January 1, 1965, is similar to editorial writer Kanai's proposal for a white paper on A-bomb victims, except that the medical review will be made and reported by medical experts. Thus, in their own sphere of responsibility, the medical personnel who have been serving faithfully in Hiroshima have, through their own experience and reflection, reached a similar conclusion. Here again is testimony to the uniqueness of this 'place of destiny'. The two groups who have come up with the two plans, as their sincere human responses to the same dreadful experience, many become related to each other as Siamese twins. I personally place great hope in both groups: in coping with the extremity of human misery, they may well provide us in 1965 with a concrete basis for hope in this age of nuclear arms. The tasks they undertake constitute the only way in the twentieth anniversary year of the atomic bombings for the Japanese people to honor the dead and to respect those surviving with bitter memories. In the process, they may also bring a new and positive image to the peace movement.

# CHAPTER THREE:
# THE MORALISTS OF HIROSHIMA
## September 1964

In talking with A-bomb victims in various hospitals, in their homes, and on the streets of Hiroshima, and hearing what they have been through and how they feel about things now, I have come to realize that they, one and all, possess unique powers of observation and expression concerning what it means to be human. I have noticed that they understand in very concrete ways such words as courage, hope, sincerity, and even 'miserable death'. The way they use these terms makes them what in Japanese has traditionally been called 'interpreters of human nature', and what today would translate as 'moralists'. The reason they became moralists is that they experienced the cruelest days in human history and have endured nineteen years since. Whenever I think of the moralists of Hiroshima, I recall first an old woman who is one of the leading members of the Hiroshima Mothers' Group which publishes the splendid small magazine, 'The Rivers of Hiroshima.' She is a woman who speaks her mind boldly, and how attractive her vivid, incisive expression is —

especially when describing the life and opinions of a certain local conservative politician who managed to rise to prominence during and after the Second World War.

I hope that readers will take what follows as an episode in a roguish novel about a fictitious person, since my purpose in introducing it here is to present this woman's interesting manner of speaking. Most probably every district of Japan has stories of similar rogue heroes. But those stories may relate to real persons, while this tale from start to finish consists of only rumor. I will therefore call my rogue hero 'Red Blood', a purely fictitious character. It is said that at the close of the war he had brought dishonor on himself as an unpatriotic person and was arrested by the military police. But he was later released, at which time he said to the people of his town, 'The blood of an unpatriotic person may not be red, but mine is red.'

Well, it is rumored that Red Blood was arrested by the military police during wartime because there were many defective shells among the munitions produced for the army by his factory. One day, when the war was at its height, an old woman (the narrator of this episode) met a farmer as she was on her way to gather mushrooms in the forest. The farmer was so excited that he foamed at the mouth; he was in a hurry to go see the rogue Red Blood executed by a firing squad. The woman, middle-aged at the time, cried out, 'I can gather mushrooms any time, but this is the only chance I'll ever have to see him shot.' She turned from her way and ran after the farmer. Fortunately, the execution was called off, and the rogue Red Blood was released, leaving his famous words.

It was after the war that Red Blood began to play an active social role. As with the rogue hero in every novel, he displayed such sexual prowess that his first nickname was 'Widow Robber'.

He next tried to enter the political arena. For that purpose he stressed that late in the war he had come close to being executed by a firing squad; that is, he tried to present himself as having been a fighter against imperialism. But this rogue was not so simple-minded as to think that he could win a local election through such an abstract tactic alone. So, with the widow who became his collaborator throughout his political career, he cleaned out all the drainage ditches in his electoral district. This clever tactic worked; he was elected and gained influence as a powerful local politician. He soon found favor among more powerful men, especially the conservatives from pre-war days, through whose support he won a seat as a conservative member of the local assembly. In that capacity, he performed well in getting helpful, concrete relief for the A-bomb victims. When various influential groups, including the progressive Japan Council against A- and H-bombs, engaged in the 'religious war of the peace movement', Red Blood gave some support to the conservatives in Hiroshima. In time, as happens with rogue heroes in novels, Red Blood acquired something of the aura of a saint. Consequently, Red Blood prospered after the war.

On the other hand, the old woman's husband, a doctor, was purged for having been a town assembly leader during the war. The old doctor lamented, 'My reputation is ruined.' He was afflicted with neurosis and, in his disappointment, took to buying all sorts of new medicines and trying them all. For several days following the atomic bombing, the aged doctor had been one of the doctors who worked devotedly to help the people of Hiroshima. As he, too, had been exposed to the atomic bomb, it was not unnatural that he should obtain and himself use sizeable quantities of each new medicine that came out as soon as he heard of it. But he indulged this interest to excess; and, according to his old wife, he died because his internal organs were eroded by the poisons produced by the reaction of all the new medicinal substances in his stomach. The old woman was also an A-bomb victim but had enjoyed good health, so she firmly refused to take any of the new medicines. Instead, she took a traditional herbal medicine, which cost her five thousand yen each month; and she criticized her husband for his indulgence. Herbal medicines are not used by the hospitals in Hiroshima for the treatment of A-bomb diseases; consequently, she could not depend upon the national assistance for medical expenses available to certified A-bomb victims. The old doctor and his old wife had both been healthy before the atomic bombing; that they both grew remarkably weaker after the bombing indicates clearly that they suffered various symptoms due to exposure to the atomic bomb, regardless of the fact that one had an obsession for new medicines and the other a preference for traditional herbals.

The truth is, though, that A-bomb victims cannot obtain certification for government medical assistance unless they have one or more of certain specific symptoms designated by the Ministry of Health and Welfare. How often I have had A-bomb victims tell me confidentially that they had no illness before the bombing and no definite symptoms of A-bomb disease afterward, yet they are certainly not in good health.[28] Thus, for the A-bomb victims, there are two conflicting factors involved: on the one hand, almost any symptom may be related to the massive and multiple impact of heat, blast, and radiation, including long-term after-effects — conditions which the human race, including the medical profession, never before experienced and has yet to comprehend fully; and, on the other hand, they cannot qualify for government protection unless their complaints fall within the rather narrow range of specified symptoms, many of which are fatal.

Now, this old woman has no connection whatsoever with any authoritarian belief or value system. She is a stubborn, independent-minded person who bases her judgments on what she sees with her own eyes and hears with her own ears. She has no use for dogmatic or conventional ideas; she has seen too many people struggle to overcome difficulties which established ideas and norms could not have solved anyway. It is people like this woman whom I call the moralists of Hiroshima. According to her, people who drowned their cares in liquor immediately after exposure to the atomic bomb did not suffer radiation illness, for the radioactivity turned to froth and oozed out of their skin.[29] Hot-bath therapy and moxa cauterization[30] of infected skin areas have been tried, with good effect, by some people. These traditional therapies cannot be simply rejected out of hand. The point is that Dr Shigeto and others of the A-bomb Hospital staff have recorded everything done in the treatment of A-bomb diseases because they were coping with unprecedented conditions; they were pioneering in virgin territory. Thus the old woman continued to speak eloquently. But when she came to reporting on fellow bomb victims with whom the Hiroshima Mothers' Group is always in contact, a certain sadness crept into her forceful expression.

A young mother, who is a friend of the old woman's

daughter, gave birth to a stillborn, deformed child. The young mother was an A-bomb victim who had suffered burns and consequent keloid scars; she had prepared herself for misfortune, but wanted to have a look at her baby. When the doctor refused to permit it, she asked her husband to look at it. He went to see the baby, only to find that it had already been disposed of. I am told that the young mother lamented, 'If only I could see my baby, I would have courage.' I was astonished by the word 'courage' in her otherwise grief-stricken and hopeless statement. The word belongs among those which have been given a new depth of meaning by the existentialists. The hospital policy of not showing deformed stillborn babies to their mothers is certainly humane. Limits need to be maintained on what we are allowed to see so that we will remain human. But if a mother wants to see her dead deformed child so as to regain her own courage, she is attempting to live at the minimum limit under which a human being can remain human. This may be interpreted as a valiant expression of humanism beyond popular humanism — a new humanism sprouting from the misery of Hiroshima. Who is not moved by the spirit of this young mother, for whom even a deformed stillborn baby would be a sign to which she could cling in order to regain her courage?

Another young mother was obsessed with anxiety throughout her pregnancy at the thought of bearing a deformed child — so much so that her fear disturbed the physical functions necessary to delivery. As a result, when her time came, her labor pains came and went, off and on, for many hours. She finally had a normal baby, but her own body never fully recovered from that time on.

Although many young mothers suffer neurosis, the fact

that they reject abortion and choose to go ahead and bear children shows the bravery of these young A-bomb victims. The overall picture, however, is not always so encouraging. Not a few couples among the A-bomb victims have divorced because they could not have children; and some young wives, compelled by those around them to appear brave, must struggle secretly with neuroses.

There are, of course, even sadder stories. One girl, for example, happened to see her hospital chart, on which was written 'myeloid leukemia', and then hanged herself. Whenever I hear such stories, I feel we are fortunate that ours is not a Christian country. I feel an almost complete relief that a dogmatic Christian sense of guilt did not prevent the girl from taking her own life. None of us survivors can morally blame her. We have only the freedom to remember the existence of 'people who do not kill themselves in spite of their misery.' My personal feeling about myself is that I, as a Japanese, might be the kind of person who, if attacked by cancer, would hang himself without any sense of guilt or fear of hell. At least, I doubt that I am qualified to prevent others from committing suicide. I am, as it were, too corroded by a sort of spiritless mold. Being such a person, I regain courage when I encounter the thoroughly and fundamentally human sense of morality in the Hiroshima people 'who do not kill themselves in spite of their misery.'

The political scandal in the newspapers this third week of September as I write this section opens with a sensational account of Khrushchev's statement that the Russians now possess 'a fearful weapon capable of exterminating mankind.' Several days later this was revised as 'fearful new-style weapons,' using the plural form. However wide the gap between the two expressions may be, I cannot rid myself of the impression that these awesome weapons reign over our age like raving-mad gods. In this nuclear age, should not the morality of 'people who do not kill themselves in spite of their misery' apply universally to us all? Certainly we share naturally the morality of people in Hiroshima who were unavoidably degraded and, yet, did not commit suicide.

In another suicide case, an old man who had been in a ward in a charity institution in Hiroshima's suburbs threw himself from a ferry boat into the Inland Sea, leaving only an A-bomb victim's health book. This old man had no objective symptoms of A-bomb disease, but for a long time had suffered mental distress, or what is known as 'A-bomb neurosis'. I am not so robustly normal as to be capable of regarding it as abnormal for people who spend their solitary later years in Hiroshima to succumb to such neurotic conditions.

Several years ago, a series of articles entitled 'Testimonies of Hiroshima' appeared daily over a period extending from A-bomb memorial day to some time after that. One article told about an old man who lapsed into an abyss worse than suicide. He was eighty-seven years old at the time he was visited by a reporter. His grandson had died of an A-bomb disease three years prior to this visit, and the old man had lost his sanity. As the youngster's parents had already died, the old man had brought up his grandson. The young man had entered a university in Tokyo but, due to financial difficulty, had left school and returned to Hiroshima. Soon after, he met a painful death in the A-bomb Hospital. Because the old man had been unable to send money to his grandson, the young man had been forced to look for a job; but he was not physically able to endure working. Following his return to Hiroshima, he was always tired and spent much time in bed. The young man began to lose his eyesight, and so went to a doctor, who found that not only his eyes but also his kidneys were affected, and his white cell count was low. He soon lost his sight entirely, due to hemorrhage of the eye ground. A month later, he began to vomit blood and, due to intense pain, wept frequently. Then, suddenly one day, he became quiet and complained, 'I am so lonely, so lonely.' He then breathed his last, after crying out, 'Ahh! Ahh! Ahh!' It was an extremely cruel death.

For a long time after his grandson's death, the old man spent many days sitting silently before the family altar. Then, all of a sudden, one day he began to talk endlessly to his grandson. 'You said you had no money, not even ten yen. My dear Takashi, it must have been miserable for you.' The old man's memories of the youth always involved money and the wretchedness of poverty. 'When you said you wanted to sell your bicycle, I should have let you, without getting angry. Takashi, my boy, I'm sure you needed the money. Oh, poor boy!' He always thought of the boy as burdened with the 'wretchedness of poverty.' Is there any more miserable despair from which it is absolutely impossible to recover than forever to reproach oneself for causing another's misery? In his own mind the old man constantly saw the simplified image of the young boy standing by his bicycle, which he was forbidden to sell, in the bombed-out wasteland of death and desolation, always feeling wretched because he lacked money, even ten yen; and alongside that image, he saw another —

himself, unreasonably enraged, refusing to let the boy sell his bicycle.

The old man related the following to the reporter:

My dear Takashi said to me, 'I will die before you do, Grandpa. So, come along to where I'm going now; and don't worry about losing your way.' When it's your time to go, there is no point in talking about the atomic bomb. If Mr Tojo had died earlier, then my dear Takashi would not have had to die. My dead Takashi said so; and he also said, 'I wanted to phone you, but I had no money, not even ten yen,' and then he slipped and fell under the eaves of the roof.

The reporter could no longer understand what the old man was saying. The man returned to conversing with his dead grandson, saying, 'When you said you wanted to sell your bicycle. . . .'

Confronted by the reporter, a stranger, the mad old man returned to the real world for a little while. His manner of speaking during the brief time was curious; it had the formal style of an orator addressing a great crowd. The old man had been a foreman in a supply depot during the war, and in his entire life had probably never had a chance to make a speech to a group of people unknown to himself. He had resolved to tell someone else about his dead grandson at some time. What he wanted to say had already taken on the style of a formal speech and was stored in his consciousness awaiting delivery. 'There is no point in talking about the atomic bomb. If Mr Tojo [war-time prime minister] had died earlier, then my dear Takashi would not have had to die.'

In this sense it may be said, 'That style is the man.' The

old man's speech was so short that it took only a few seconds out of his whole lifetime, but the necessity to express himself was so intense that only the style of formal speech sufficed. Such a speech touches our hearts. In our time speeches are too long and grandiose yet too void of content to compare with the old man's. I shall never forget his few lines.

In Hiroshima this summer I asked many people about this old man. Some said that he had died; others, that he still carries on endless conversations with his dead grandson about the shameful experiences of poverty. In Hiroshima, the seasons of human life and death flow by swiftly. In the 'Testimonies of Hiroshima' series, I read also about an old Korean woman who lost her five children in the atomic blast and herself suffered terrible keloid scars from chest to neck and on both arms. She lived in an old shack, where she put up a signboard with the words 'Hiroshima Korean Branch of the Japan Holiness Church.' Children in the streets called her a 'mad Korean granny.' At one time in her life she had fallen into despair; she cursed America for dropping the atomic bomb and hated Japan for starting the war. 'If I had not been given the grace of God, I would have killed myself or gone crazy.' Believing in God, she managed to live normally and to maintain a small, poor church.

Now I do not curse America or hate Japan. I would like, rather, to express my gratitude to the Japanese people, because I am able to make a living and live safely in this country, despite my being Korean and even though I was disfigured by the war. Beyond that, I only want to appeal for the prohibition of atomic and hydrogen bombs. This I want to do because I am a mother who lost five children; it has nothing to do with whether I am Korean or Japanese.

I walked along the bank of the Tenmagawa River in the vicinity of Kusunoki township, searching for the shanty church of this singularly generous old Korean woman. But most of the shacks had been pulled down, and a bulldozer was clearing the area. The only makeshift structure that remained was a junkyard shed, where people, unable to bear the intense heat, were napping in their underclothes. I left there and strolled aimlessly through the overgrown summer grass. By now, no one in the neighborhood knew anything about this Korean woman with the beautiful Christian spirit.

I wish to record also a kindness that a boy of the same nationality performed soon after the atomic bomb fell. To this time no one, including the Japanese woman whose life he saved, knows where he is. He seems to have disappeared. The following episode is quoted from the memoirs of Kunie Hashimoto, who was thirty years old when she was exposed to the atomic bomb at a place 1.7 kilometers from the explosion point.

In the evening of the third day after the bombing, the sun was shining brightly, and it was unbearably hot. A boy of fourteen or fifteen — perhaps just passing by — ran up to me, looked me in the face, and said, 'There is a first-aid station over at Gongesan. Do you want to go there?' From the accent of his gasping speech, I could tell at once that he was Korean. When I nodded to accept the kind offer of this boy, whose sincerity transcended the prejudice my people harbor toward his, he took me to the first-aid station, virtually carrying me on his back; and before I realized it, he had vanished like the wind, without giving me his name and address.

The 'Testimonies of Hiroshima' also tell about a most defiant man, quite different from the old man who drowned himself by jumping off the ferry boat and from the mad old man who talked incessantly to his dead grandson. This defiant man tried to commit ritual suicide by disemboweling himself in front of the Memorial Cenotaph — not from despair but from the thought that 'if I, who am old and disabled, sacrifice myself, then the sensation may help to prevent nuclear testing.' But the small knife, which he had gone to the trouble of obtaining, would not cut through the skin of his abdomen. The old man exclaimed, 'I don't want to live a life of shame,' and tried to slit his throat. But, again, he was unable to end his life, for he was already too weakened by an A-bomb disease caused by residual radiation. He had an unusually keen sense of shame and, while lying abed in the A-bomb Hospital, repeated over and over that he had exposed himself to ridicule. It was in the gloomy September of 1961, when Khrushchev had announced the resumption of Soviet nuclear testing and the Japan Council against Atomic and Hydrogen Bombs had lacked the courage to protest Khrushchev's statement, that the old man had made up his mind to kill himself. People whom I met in Hiroshima this summer had no recent information on this stubborn and solitary old man who was never interested in talking with other patients on his ward. That is, no one knew whether he was even alive, or whether he is still burdened with a sense of humiliation for having 'exposed himself to ridicule', and with pent-up anger at the resumption of nuclear testing. The only clear information is that the nine letters of protest which the old man had prepared at the time of his suicide attempt have been ignored by the Soviet and American embassies and all other places to which he sent them.

The preceding examples are typical of the problems of elderly A-bomb victims in Hiroshima — people who lost their families in the atomic bombing and since then have survived alone in generally serious circumstances. One movement to deal with these problems is based in the Hiroshima Ikoi no Ie (Hiroshima Home), a relief facility for solitary aged victims. I have previously written about old patients who, if they get better, have no place to go upon leaving the A-bomb Hospital, and about the various threats of cancer they face, especially cancer symptoms that clearly stem from having been exposed to the atomic bomb. I have also mentioned the grievous lament: 'One old person survives alone, while the young are all dead.' How many times I have heard chagrin expressed in Hiroshima concerning this inversion of natural death, though the look in the eyes of those who lament this inversion is not so much grief or anger as it is, I dare say, a kind of shame. And I personally find this shame very disturbing.

In the tenth issue of 'Rivers of Hiroshima,' there are stories of three other ordinary old A-bomb victims who patiently rebuilt their lives without killing themselves or going crazy. Of course, their remarkable patience, which gives a calmness to their speech, can hardly be called 'ordinary' as compared with people in general.

I am seventy-two years old this year. At the time of the atomic bombing, I was working in a butchery near the

Otagawa Canal in western Hiroshima. I heard a great *dokan* [bang] sound, and in an instant was blown flat on my back on the concrete floor. Owing to the summer heat, I was wearing only a work apron over a sleeveless undershirt; and in the butchery we went barefooted, so many glass splinters stuck in my feet. Even though I was unconscious, I kept hearing a strange sound.

In late November of 1946, my eyes suddenly began to hurt intensely. I went to a hospital in the city, but gradually lost my sight anyway. I visited a number of doctors near the city, but it was already too late.

Before the bombing, I had never taken a dose of medicine. After the bombing, I grew weaker and weaker until, finally, last December, I was operated on for a liver ailment and for appendicitis. The operation revealed that my pancreas was not well. Meantime, construction work had begun on the Otagawa Canal, and the city was laying a streetcar line through my neighborhood, so I had to move. I don't know how many times I thought of killing myself; but I said to myself that it was useless to die and decided not to commit suicide.

A former butcher, whose wife had died, had to live alone when his only relative, a nephew paralyzed from infancy, got married and left him. He expressed his gratitude humorously: 'As I suffer from blindness, people give me various things and bring me cigarettes, saying, "I picked up a good one on the street."'

A solitary woman of seventy-four who teaches the koto (long Japanese zither) says:

I had been taught to play the koto using written music; so I can recall the technique even now if I look at the musical score. I now teach koto to others, for I think that teaching is a good way of reviewing what I once learned. When playing the koto I am so happy because I needn't think of anything else. The house I rent is quite convenient, as I can come and go from the rear entrance. I spend a lot of time training my dog Bill. Since the bombing I have learned that even if we lose everything, we gain something.

Another woman of the same age says of herself:

I think walking is best for my health. When I have nothing else to do, I just walk about, here and there. Some people tell me, 'You are a great walker.' My husband died in Manchuria; my younger sister died in Okinawa; her eldest son was killed in battle in Central China, and her second son is enshrined in the Memorial Monument dedicated to students of Okinawa Normal School who were killed in the war. I now live on a government livelihood allowance and supplement my income by going on errands for others or by looking after houses while the owners are away. The regular radio subscriber's fee[31] is the hardest thing for me to squeeze from my meager resources. Now I hope to realize my final wish to visit the Memorial Monument in Okinawa where my nephew is enshrined.

I think we should call these solitary, old A-bomb victims 'people who do not pity themselves in spite of everything.' If the blind former butcher's decision not to commit suicide can be ascribed to his strong will, so the courage of the women in their seventies can be said to derive from their belonging to a group of A-bomb victims and to the liberation of self from suicidal tendencies that such belonging can give.

The old woman koto teacher confides, 'I was all alone, but have found friends since joining the A-bomb Victims Association.' And the old woman who keeps healthy by walking reports, 'After I joined the A-bomb Victims Association in Minami township of Hiroshima City in 1960, the loneliness of my solitary life disappeared. In our meetings we can talk together without reservation about our sorrows and joys, and funds sent by distant, unknown people are distributed among us. When I am in touch with the warm hearts of others this way, I feel that I receive courage to go on living as long as I can.' The word 'courage' as used by these solitary elderly victims, as in the case of the young mother of the dead deformed child, possesses real moral force, though the nuances vary somewhat.

In the preceding essay I mentioned the few brief sentences left behind by Mr Sadao Miyamoto, the 'last man' in the A-bomb Hospital who maintained such a strong interest in the peace movement. He was also a man of courage who, like the solitary aged victims, deserves to be included among the 'people who did not kill themselves in spite of everything.' He was the sort of person who, if an inpatient of the hospital did anything slovenly, always became upset and made his complaint known. He had more self-respect than the other patients — one of whom lamented his passing by saying, 'Mr Miyamoto, you were dictatorial and fastidious, but you were sincere.'

The reason that he always complained may be that he did not consider himself merely an inpatient in the A-bomb Hospital, a recluse separated from the real world. He found a real world among the patients and involved himself positively in it. Accordingly, while he was not responsible for the administration of the hospital, he nonetheless 'admonished patients not to use the hospital tableware in their rooms without permission and warned them strictly about turning off the gas in the service room after use.' He also possessed considerable manual dexterity; he made a model castle with matchsticks and cardboard, and a figure of the legendary hero, Taro Urashima, with small shells and painted it with gold dust. His character, which made him live each day with perseverance, was not that of a desperate person. But eventually his skillful hands grew cold as ice, and he had to wear gloves even indoors. He could no longer enjoy handicrafts.

When referring earlier to his final statement, I focused on his phrase, 'people who go on struggling toward a miserable death.' As I noted then, this does not mean to struggle in order to die, or to try to keep from dying, or even to struggle to gain new life; it means to struggle along the way toward a miserable death, or until meeting a miserable death. I do not think that Mr Miyamoto (who has by now met his own miserable death) made a mistake in using the preposition 'toward' in the last statement of his life. He probably chose the words 'people who go on struggling toward a miserable death' as most suitable for expressing his own feelings. As I understand it, Mr Miyamoto left this phrase with the strongest sense of humanism, for he did not himself lose courage even while struggling for nothing more than to give meaning to the time until his own death came. It is just this understanding that the existentialists first made clear. In this sense, Mr

Miyamoto is representative of the moralists of Hiroshima.

If ever we experience another massive nuclear flash and thunder over our heads again, I am sure that the morality for survival when surrounded by death and desolation will need to draw on the wisdom of those who, through their bitter experiences in Hiroshima, became the first moralists, or 'interpreters of human nature', in our nuclear age.

If the human race is fortunate enough never to experience an attack by nuclear weapons again, still the wisdom of the Hiroshima people who survived the worst days of human experience must certainly be cherished.

What must we do to preserve and pass on the true morality of the taciturn people in Hiroshima — where it is already difficult to seek out the moralists, even with the help of news stories written only a few years ago? What must we begin to do right away? No doubt the preparation of a white paper on A-bomb victims and damages, to mark the twentieth anniversary of the atomic bombings, would contribute much to the preservation and promotion of that precious morality.

# CHAPTER FOUR:
# ON HUMAN DIGNITY
## October 1964

In this age of nuclear weapons, when their power gets more attention than the misery they cause, and when human events increasingly revolve around their production and proliferation, what must we Japanese try to remember? Or more pointedly, what must I myself remember and keep on remembering?

Until only yesterday, a great nation that had recently acquired the power to possess nuclear weapons, chose not to do so. So long as it could but did not, it projected an image of a nation that could take the lead in producing new political ideas and ideals in this nuclear age. But now, in October 1964, as I write this note, the People's Republic of China no longer has that valuable image. Overnight it has become a different country.

In such a time as this, I want to remember, and keep on remembering, the thoughts of the people of Hiroshima — the first people and the first place to experience full force the world's worst destructive capability. Hiroshima is like a nakedly exposed wound inflicted on all mankind. Like all wounds, this one also poses two potential outcomes: the hope of human recovery, and the danger of fatal corruption. Unless we persevere in remembering the Hiroshima experience, especially the thoughts of those who underwent that unprecedented experience, the faint signs of recovery emerging from this place and people will begin to decay and real degeneration will set in.

As one who has often visited Hiroshima, I am concerned to record what I learned there, along with my personal reflections on that city and its citizens. This note, like the others, is written rather hastily in sketchy, outline form, as it is foremost for my own task of remembering. Since the middle of the night when China began its nuclear test, I have frequently been kept awake till dawn by telephone calls from news agencies. But in this note I am not responding to their questions; I choose, rather, to put down my own thoughts, because I want to reconstruct my own image of Hiroshima.

In this essay, therefore, I will focus on human dignity, for it is the most important thing I have discovered in Hiroshima, and it is precisely what I need to support and direct my own life. I say that I discovered human dignity in Hiroshima, but that does not necessarily mean that I can explain it well or accurately. Indeed, words do not suffice, for the reality of human dignity transcends language. I have sensed this since my childhood. It will be easier if I try to be concrete, though I am not sure that concreteness will convey adequately and generally my understanding of human dignity. I can only try.

I have already written, for example, about the stubborn resistance of an angry old man who attempted suicide to protest the resumption of nuclear testing; of how his suicide attempt failed and his protest was ignored; and of how he finally felt exposed to dishonor. I think that he surely had human dignity, despite his sense of failure. It is dignity like his that captivates my mind. To put it bluntly, he was left with nothing but human dignity. When I think of the old man's failed suicide, his ignored protest, his long time abed in the hospital, and then try to identify what significance such a life had, the answer is clear: the value of his life lay precisely in the human dignity that he achieved in his miserable old age. Reduced to lying in a hospital bed with a big scar on his abdomen, still he could face with dignity all people without keloid scars, that is to say, all people everywhere who had no experience of the atomic bomb. This is one example of what I mean by 'human dignity'.

In the summer of 1963 when I saw Mr Miyamoto make his welcome speech to the peace marchers, I noted that he 'withdrew with evident satisfaction and dignity.' At the time I knew nothing about this small, middle-aged man other than that he represented the other patients and that he said, 'I believe the Ninth World Conference will be a success,' in a strained, mosquito-like voice while standing in the bright summer sunshine. Nevertheless, I sensed that he was full of unmistakable dignity.

After that, I often wrote the word 'dignity' in my notebooks on Hiroshima. I found dignity in the old philosopher who was a leader in the peace movement; and also in his wife, who had something of the young girl in her. And I found dignity as well in the old lady who was a key member of the group that publishes the 'Rivers of Hiroshima' series and who criticized the influential conservatives of Hiroshima in her bold, humorous manner of speaking. Theirs is just the sort of dignity that I find most human. It is, in fact, the kind of dignity that I have been longing for since my childhood, though I have never been sure that I could attain it someday. Now I realize that the inner impulse compelling me to visit Hiroshima so often has been the sense of dignity I find in the people there.

Clearly, I encountered such dignity in Dr Shigeto, director of the A-bomb Hospital. It has nothing to do with the fact that he is the director of the hospital; I found the same dignity in Mr Miyamoto, a patient of the hospital. Originally I had intended to make use of public surveys to provide in these notes my personal summary of the history of medical care extended to the A-bomb victims. The leading role in A-bomb medical care, however, was not taken by the national government; quite the opposite, it was started with virtually no initial resources through the energy and efforts of the unbowing, persevering local people who had to contend with reluctant national authorities every step of the way.[32] If one reviews the role of the Atomic Bomb Casualty Commission, backed by the occupation forces, along with the conservative government of Japan, it will be clear that medical care for A-bomb victims has been sustained primarily by the strength of local and regional organizations, and that local leaders often had to cope with recalcitrant national agencies.

The A-bomb Hospital was not built by, nor is it maintained by, the national government. It was built with proceeds from the New Year's postal lottery[33] distributed to Hiroshima Red Cross Hospital. The director, Dr Shigeto, an A-bomb victim himself, has from that first miserable moment to the present time devoted himself completely to providing proper medical care and to analyzing A-bomb effects, even to the extent of peddling his bicycle among the ruins to collect fragments of irradiated tiles. The dignity I saw in this devoted man was that of an unadorned, unpretentious man. He strives to do his best, but he does not appeal to or rely on external authority. Where did these dignified people come from? I dare say their dignity is not the simple kind generally found anywhere.

To clarify my use of the word 'dignity', I want first of all to explain how I came to use it, how it became a part of my vocabulary. To do so is to share some of my personal experiences and reflections from childhood to the present. The idea of dignity began to attract me during the Second World War, when I was still quite young; and later, when I was a university student reading French wartime literature, the term haunted me even more and assumed more definite meaning.

At first I had only a simple awareness of something with great meaning, but knew no word for it. Toward the end of the war, I was a young boy in a mountain village on Shikoku Island; and I suffered a terrible dilemma, the cause of which was an episode in a movie I had seen at the village theater. In the episode, a young soldier was captured by the enemy; afraid that he might confess a military secret, he committed suicide at once. I shuddered, terribly moved and trembling with fear. I had a premonition that I, too, would surely be reduced to a similar extremity during the war. It became for me a pressing matter to decide what I would then do. While I was deeply moved by the soldier's action, I also doubted, as a terrified child with a selfish love of my own life, that anything was so important to me that I would risk or give my life for it. A newcomer in this world with no reason to leave it, I felt an unspeakable fear of my own death. If I were threatened with death unless I revealed a secret, if I were faced with a choice between life and death, I would readily confess any secret like a coward. Would I ever become a person who would not surrender even though threatened with death or who would resist unto death? Concealing my inner dilemma behind a child's innocent expression, I asked my father (who saw the movie with me) why the young soldier had committed suicide. Father's reply was a short, shocking one, the likes of which I had till then never heard from an adult's lips. It was an irritated father's punishment of a boy's disguised innocence.

'That soldier? He would surely have been killed after being forced to confess, even if he had not committed suicide.'

Did my father hope by this to still my mind, upset as it was by the soldier's death? The soldier would die after all, so it was all the same, anyway. But I began to fear anew, terribly, the situation in which the soldier would die after all. I, too, would probably be the kind who is killed after confessing. Already deeply moved by one who could commit suicide without confessing a secret, I felt disgusted with the type of person who would confess and die anyway. Still, I could not be taught by anyone, not even my father, how to change my cowardly nature to one capable of committing suicide. With childlike vanity, I conjured up various scenarios. I imagined my future comrades; and to save them, I would picture myself committing suicide — but, even in fantasy, I wound up at the wall for execution. How could I put the lives of others above my own death?

Was not my death final and absolute? In father's terms, my death would surely come without relation to the death of others. Before falling into such an extremity (which, as I said earlier, I felt was my destiny sooner or later), I prayed that I could somehow persuade myself to change from the disgusting, cowardly type to the admirable, courageous type who could kill himself.

The war ended while I was still a child, so the battlefield decision was, so to speak, postponed. Yet I continued to wonder if I were one who could die unsurrendered or merely one who would be killed after surrendering. The dilemma lingered long after I was free of any real possibility of being sent off to war. I struck inward. Sometimes I longed to do something violent; at times I fancied myself a masochist. I was such a strange student. I entered the department of literature and began reading modern French literature. In my classes I observed that, as in Japanese literature, French literature has certain special modes of expression; I was especially interested in synonymous words in the two languages that appeared with high frequency in French works but were virtually absent from Japanese works. The following are two such words that attracted my attention:

dignity (*dignité*)

humiliation, or shame (*humiliation, honte*)

The terms, or concepts, had been associated with my terrible dilemma since childhood. The ghosts of the two words never ceased to haunt me. I do not, of course, claim that such words have never been used in Japanese literature. Indeed, it is not amiss to say that 'humiliation' and 'shame' are traditional themes in our autobiographical novels. But in French literature, the words 'humiliation' and 'shame' are the sharpest moral barbs to pierce the heart of both author and reader. These words never appear in Japanese literature with the same weight and force. The matter is even clearer in the case of the other word, 'dignity'. The sentence 'That boy is full of dignity,' for example, does not flow naturally in Japanese syntax. It sounds like a sentence translated from a foreign language.

In time I learned to express my childhood dilemma more clearly, as 'When will I change from one who might be killed after being humiliated or shamed, to one who might kill himself with dignity?' Of course, in the passage from youth to adulthood, I have not retained the habit of thinking in such extreme terms. It is too childish. But the terms 'dignity', 'humiliation', and 'shame', which came into my vocabulary this way, are still the most essential terms to me. I saw things related to the worst sort of humiliation in Hiroshima; but for the first time in my life I saw there the most dignified Japanese people. Moreover, the words 'dignity', 'humiliation', and 'shame' are not such simple terms in the context of the place where the cruelest experience of human history occurred. At least, these words always possess a deeper meaning in that context.

As for humiliation and shame, we can recall the old man who protested the resumption of nuclear tests by attempting self-disembowelment but failed, and thus felt miserably shamed. His sense of shame itself, however, gives substance to his sense of dignity. So it is with the solitary old A-bomb victims who, ashamed to survive when the young die, speak of this with dignity as an 'inversion'. A young woman, with whom I became acquainted at the A-bomb Hospital and met there again a year later, told me that she was ashamed of herself; and it is in Hiroshima that a great many girls stay indoors because they are ashamed of the ugly keloid scars on their faces. How can we understand the sense of shame that the A-bomb victims feel about their experiences, without also being ashamed of ourselves? What a frightening inversion of feeling!

A girl is ashamed of her face disfigured by keloids. In her mind she divides all people on earth into two groups; the sense of shame is the line separating persons with keloid scars from all others without them. The girls with keloids feel ashamed of themselves before those who have none. They feel humiliated by curious glances of all other people who have no keloid disfigurations.

What life-styles have the girls with keloids chosen so as to cope with their burden of shame and humiliation? One of their ways of coping is to keep away from others' eyes, hiding themselves in the dark recesses of their homes. Those who escape this way are probably the most numerous. Staying quietly in the back rooms of their homes, they are now losing their youth. All others — the non-escapists — may naturally be divided into two groups. One of these groups includes all who want atomic bombs dropped again so that all people on the earth will suffer the same keloids as themselves. The burden of shame would be easier to bear if shared by everyone. People would stop staring at the keloid-scarred girls with the eyes of 'others', for there would then be no 'others'. The division most loathsome to the girls would have disappeared from the earth. I have, in fact, heard such a wish voiced, and in an earlier essay quoted a short poem that expresses the same feeling (see p. 61). This wish, this curse on the world, is actually no more than longing for psychological support in coping with their burdens. Most of these girls have become silent and, indeed, should be classed among the escapists.

There is yet another group. They are people who take the misery inflicted upon them by the atomic bomb and convert it from a passive into an active force; they use their shame and humiliation as weapons in the movement against nuclear arms.

This rather strained division of mine, however, is really unnecessary. Hiroshima as a whole must exert all its energy to articulate the essential intellectual grounds for abolishing all nuclear weapons in such a way that all of the victims' dehumanizing experiences — the misery, the shame and humiliation, the meanness and degradation — may be converted into things of worth so that the human dignity of the A-bomb victims may be restored. All people with keloids and all without keloids must together affirm this effort. What other human means can there be for liberating the A-bomb victims from their tragic fear of a miserable death?

Even if, through some *political* arrangement, all nuclear weapons were abolished, it would be useless for restoring the humanity of the A-bomb victims. I hold this simple principle to be axiomatic from moral and intellectual perspectives. And, I wish to reaffirm here, it applies to China's nuclear armament as well. Will anyone regard this way of thinking as sentimental? If you yourself had ugly keloid scars and wanted to overcome the mental anguish they cause, would you, too, not believe that your own keloid ugliness might have some value in the cause of eliminating all nuclear weapons? Is not such belief the only way to transform the pain and fear of dying in vain of leukemia into something worthwhile?

In the broadest context of human life and death, those of us who happened to escape the atomic holocaust must see Hiroshima as part of all Japan, and as part of all the world. If we survivors want to atone for the 'Hiroshima' within us and to give it some positive value, then we should mobilize all efforts against nuclear arms under the maxims 'the human misery of Hiroshima' and 'the restoration of all humanity'. Some people may hold to the fairy-tale view, in this highly politicized age, that the new acquisition of nuclear arms by one country actually advances the cause of nuclear disarmament. Since the world has in fact taken the initial step forward in that direction, there may be some ultimate possibility of completely eradicating nuclear weapons.

I cannot, however, overlook the fact that the first actual step toward the non-nuclear dream has virtually crushed the hope for self-recovery of the girls who, ashamed of their keloids, are presently wasting their youth in the dark back rooms of Hiroshima. Moreover, there is no clear prospect of the complete abolition of nuclear arms. How harsh this situation is for the people of Hiroshima! I hardly have the nerve to probe their feelings.

To put the matter plainly and bluntly, people everywhere on this earth are trying to forget Hiroshima and the unspeakable tragedy perpetrated there. We naturally try to forget our personal tragedies, serious or trifling, as soon as possible (even something as petty as being scorned or disdained by a stranger on a street corner). We try not to carry these things over to tomorrow. It is not strange, therefore, that the whole human race is trying to put Hiroshima, the extreme point of human tragedy, completely out of mind. Without bothering to thumb through public school textbooks, we know that grown-ups make no effort to convey their memories of Hiroshima to their children. All who fortunately survived, or at least luckily suffered no radiation injury, seek to forget the ones who, even now, are struggling painfully *toward* death. Forgetting all these things, we go on living comfortably in the crazy world of the late twentieth century.

In October 1964, when a young man born in Hiroshima on the A-bomb day was selected as the last runner to carry the Olympic flame,[34] an American journalist — who has translated some Japanese literature and might be expected to understand Japan and the Japanese people — publicly stated his opinion that this was an unhappy choice because it reminded the Americans of the atomic bomb. If the selected runner had had keloid scars or some other sign of radiation injury, that is, if he had been an unmistakable A-bomb casualty, then I would not object to the selection; an A-bomb victim (if fortunate enough to have lived for these twenty years) would have been more representative of those born on the day of the atomic bombing. But the middle-distance runner actually chosen had a perfectly healthy body; we were impressed by his stamina as he ran at full speed in the huge stadium, with the smile of one free of all anxiety. I blessed this young man's perfectly healthy body for the sake of Dr Shigeto who is already at work on the 'problem of the next generation of A-bomb victims.'

Still, the American journalist was displeased because the young man, born in Hiroshima on the atomic bombing day, reminded Americans of the atomic bomb. He preferred to erase all traces of Hiroshima from the American memory. Worse still, this preference occurs not only to the American mind. Do not all leaders and peoples who at present possess nuclear weapons also wish to erase Hiroshima from their memories? As the white paper on A-bomb victims and damages seeks to make clear, Hiroshima is the prime example not of the power of atomic weapons but of the misery they cause. But we want to put that aside and get on with living. This attitude is common around the world. Powerful leaders in the East and in the West insist on maintaining nuclear arms as a means of preserving the peace. There may be some room for various observations and rationales regarding the possible usefulness of nuclear weapons in preserving true peace; indeed, printing presses all over the world are running off such arguments with all haste. But it is obvious that all advocates of usefulness base their opinions on the *power* of nuclear arms. Such is the fashion and common sense of today's world. Who, then, would want to remember Hiroshima as the extremity of human misery?

Not infrequently I encounter A-bomb victims in Hiroshima who say that they want to forget the atomic bomb and do not want to discuss its awesome blast and flash. As for the Olympic flame case, if anyone has the right to protest that the selected runner was an unpleasant reminder of the atomic bomb, the bomb's victims can lay first claim to that right. More than anyone, they would like to forget the horrors of that day. Indeed, they need to forget in order to get on with everyday living. In university I had a friend from Hiroshima; and during our four years together, I never heard him talk about the atomic bomb. Of course, he had a right to remain silent about it.

In Hiroshima at dawn on A-bomb Memorial Day, I have often seen many women standing silently, with deep, dark, fearful eyes, at the Memorial Cenotaph and similar places. On such occasions, I recalled some lines by the Russian poet Yevtushenko [Yevgeny, 1933-]:[35]

> Her motionless eyes had no expression;
> Yet there was something there, sorrow
> 
> or agony,
> Inexpressible,
> but something terrible.

Had I spoken to the women, they would have remained silent. They, too, have a right to silence. They have the right, if possible, to forget everything about Hiroshima. They have had enough of Hiroshima. Some A-bomb victims, knowing that the best medical treatment of A-bomb symptoms is available in Hiroshima, nonetheless choose to live elsewhere because they want to get away from all that Hiroshima represents, inwardly and outwardly. Again, they have the right, if possible, to escape Hiroshima completely.

If, however, a victim develops symptoms of an A-bomb related disease, then he can neither forget nor escape Hiroshima. He can, of course, live without thinking about Hiroshima, as far as possible, even if he is a patient in the A-bomb Hospital. If, in addition to removing Hiroshima entirely from his consciousness, the patient could recover fully and move far away from Hiroshima, never to return again, he would be most fortunate. Indeed, if all patients could do so, how wonderful it would be!

Mr Sadao Miyamoto, however, was a patient who participated in the anti-nuclear movement at risk to his already fragile life. He consciously accepted Hiroshima. He dared to remember history's worst human misery, and he wrote down his reflections on it. He spoke freely, but with some humor, about it to foreigners who frequently visited the hospital. Rather than escape Hiroshima, he accepted it. For whose sake? For the sake of all other human beings, for all who would remain after he met his own miserable death. His passion stemmed from his frank recognition that his own death was inevitable. Mr Sankichi Toge, that excellent poet, also died in Hiroshima; it was after he had a hemorrhage of the lungs (eventually fatal) that he participated passionately in political activities. 'The cruel lung hemorrhage suffered by Mr Toge in April 1949 made him struggle against the terror of death . . . [and] decide to join the Japan Communist Party' (testimony of Mr Kiyoshi Toyota).

If survivors would overcome their fear of death, they too must see some way of giving meaning to their own death. Thus, the dead can survive as part of the lives of those who still live. Gambling on life after death and taking an active role in the hospital was the way taken by Mr Miyamoto; political participation and joining the Communist Party was Mr Toge's way. What terrifies me is that we are completely wasting their death gambles. Mr Miyamoto seems to have suspected that we would. It bothers me no end to think of this waste. And do not we survivors refuse to gamble on our deaths for fear that we will have to pay off as losers?

Instead of 'the dead', I prefer to call these people 'saints'. They had no religion, and the poet was a Communist. But I think the term 'saint' is appropriate for them, in the sense that Albert Camus once put it. 'I am intrigued by the question of how I can become a saint.' 'But you don't believe in God, do you?' 'So, can one become a saint without God's help? — that's the only concrete question I know today.'

If there are those who dislike the word 'saint', then I do not mind remembering these two men, who refused to keep silent unto death, in terms of the following lines by Céline, written in a tougher vein:[36]

The ultimate defeat is, in short, to forget; especially to forget those who kill us. It is to die without any suspicion, to the very end, of how perverse people are. There is no use in struggling when we already have one foot in the grave. And we must not forgive and forget. We must report, one by one, everything we have learned about the cruelty of man. Otherwise, we cannot die. If we do this, then our lives will not have been wasted.

People who continue to live in Hiroshima, instead of keeping silent or forgetting about the extreme tragedy of human history, are trying to speak about it, study it, and record it. It is a formidable task, calling for extraordinary effort. Outsiders can hardly comprehend the scope and intensity of the Hiroshima people's feelings — including the personal aversion to public exposure which they must conquer in order to carry out this task. The people who stick by the city are the only ones with a right to forget it and keep silent about it; but they are the very ones who choose to discuss, study, and record it energetically.

The women of the 'Rivers of Hiroshima' series, the advocates of the A-bomb white paper, the doctors of the A-bomb Hospital, and all the victims who ever talked about their own bitter experiences and about the Hiroshima within themselves — how modest and restrained they are in making their testimony. It is by no means strange that all these Hiroshima people should possess an unmistakable dignity. Only through lives like theirs do dignified people emerge in our society.

Not since I first felt, as a child, the dilemma of how to achieve dignity have I ever attempted to write, even for practice, an essay to resolve the issue. But I think that I have learned one sure way to protect myself from feeling shame or humiliation. And that way is to endeavor never to lose sight of the dignity of people in Hiroshima.

# CHAPTER FIVE:
# THE UNSURRENDERED PEOPLE
## November 1964

Few people today view the world in terms of a dualism of good and evil. Certainly it is no longer fashionable to do so. But, all of a sudden one summer, an absolute evil intruded into the lives and consciousness of the A-bomb victims. To counter that absolute evil, it became necessary to have an absolute good in order to recover a human balance in the world and to persevere in resisting that evil. From the instant the atomic bomb exploded, it became the symbol of all human evil; it was a savagely primitive demon and a most modern curse. The attempt to accord it positive value as a means of ending the war quickly did not, however, bring peace even to the minds of all the airmen who carried out the atomic attack. The atomic bomb embodied the absolute evil of war, transcending lesser distinctions such as Japanese or Allies, attacker or attacked.

Even while the smoke still rose from the wasteland of total destruction, human goodwill began to go into action as people made their first moves toward recovery and restoration. This action was seen both in the injured victims' will to live and in the efforts of doctors who worked, in a virtual vacuum of supplies and support systems, to treat the victims. Initiated soon that summer morning by the people in Hiroshima, the acts of goodwill were essential to resisting that ultimate thrust of accumulated science which produced the atomic bomb. If one believes that there is some kind of human harmony or order in this world, then he must also believe that the efforts of the Hiroshima doctors were somehow sufficient to cope with the demonic aftermath of the atomic disaster.

For my part, I have a kind of nightmare about trusting in human strength, or in humanism; it is a nightmare about a particular kind of trust in human capability. Toward this kind of humanism (and it is nothing more than a kind of humanism), I have a strong antipathy; so much so that I cannot help thinking about it from time to time. My nightmare stems from a suspicion that a certain 'trust in human strength', or 'humanism', flashed across the minds of the American intellectuals who decided upon the project that concluded with the dropping of the atomic bomb on Hiroshima. That 'humanism' ran as follows: If this absolutely lethal bomb is dropped on Hiroshima, a scientifically predictable hell will result. But the hell will not be so thoroughly disastrous as to wipe out, once and for all, all that is good in human society. That hell will not be so completely beyond the possibility of human recovery that all mankind will despise their humanity merely at the thought of it. It will not be an unrelieved hell with no exit, or so devastatingly evil that President Truman will, throughout his life, be unable to sleep for thinking of it. There are, after all, people in Hiroshima who will make the hell as humane as they possibly can. . . . I suspect that the A-bomb planners thought in such a way; that in making the final decision, they trusted too much in the enemy's own human strength to cope with the hell that would follow the dropping of the atomic bomb. If so, theirs was a most paradoxical humanism.

Suppose that the atomic bomb had been dropped, say, on Leopoldville in the Congo, instead of on Hiroshima. Initially, a huge number of people would have died instantly; then wounded survivors, forced to accept total surrender, would have continued to die for many months to come. Epidemics would have spread, and pests would have proliferated in the desolate ruins. The city would have become a wasteland where human beings perished without cease or succor. There would have been no one to dispose of the dead. And when the victor would come in to investigate the damage — after the threat of residual radiation had passed — they would have experienced the worst nausea ever. Some of them would never be sane, normal persons again. One whole city would have been rendered as deadly as a huge death chamber in a Nazi concentration camp. All the people would have been doomed to death, with no sign of hope to be found. . . . Such a scenario is shocking to even the toughest mind. Unless some slave driver's descendant had been available to make the decision, the dropping of an atomic bomb on Leopoldville would have been postponed without setting a future date.

What actually happened in Hiroshima when the atomic bomb was in fact dropped was not quite as horrible as the preceding scenario. For one thing, the people who survived in Hiroshima made no particular effort to impress on those who dropped the bomb what a dreadful thing they had done. Even though the city was utterly devastated and had become a vast, ugly death chamber, the Hiroshima survivors first began struggling to recover and rebuild. They did so, of course, for their own sakes; but doing so served also to lessen the burden on the consciences of those who had dropped the atomic bomb.

The recovery effort has continued for two decades, and continues even now. The fact that a girl with leukemia goes on suffering all her life, not committing suicide, surely lessens — by just one person's portion — the A-bomb droppers' burden of conscience.

It is quite abnormal that people in one city should decide to drop an atomic bomb on people in another city. The scientists involved cannot possibly have lacked the ability to imagine the hell that would issue from the explosion. The decision, nevertheless, was made. I presume that it was done on the basis of some calculation of a built-in harmony by virtue of which, if the incredibly destructive bomb were dropped, the greatest effort in history would be made to counterbalance the totality of the enormous evil to follow. The inhumane damage caused by this demonic weapon would be mitigated by the humane efforts of those struggling to find what hope they could in the desperate situation.

The notion of 'balancing' also reflects a 'confidence in human strength', itself a reflection of confidence in the strength of humanism. But it is the attacking wolf's confidence in the scapegoat's ability to set things straight after the pitiless damage is done. This is the gruesome nightmare I have about humanism. Perhaps it is no more than an overanxious delusion of mine.

I think of the patience of the A-bomb victims quietly awaiting their turns in the waiting room of the Atomic Bomb Casualty Commission on the top of Hijiyama hill. At least it is true that their stoicism greatly reduces the emotional burden of the American doctors working there.

I have little knowledge of the Bible. It seems to me, though, that when God made the rain fall for forty days and nights, he fully trusted that Noah would rebuild human society after the Great Flood ended. If Noah had been a lazy man, or a hysterical man given to despair, then there would have been great consternation in God's heaven. Fortunately, Noah had the needed will and ability, so the deluge played its part within God's plan for man, without playing the tyrant beyond God's expectations. Did God, too, count on a built-in harmony of 'balancing out'? (And if so, does God not seem rather vicious?)

The atomic destruction of Hiroshima was the worst 'deluge' of the twentieth century. The people of Hiroshima went to work at once to restore human society in the aftermath of this great atomic 'flood'. They were concerned to salvage their own lives, but in the process they also salvaged the souls of the people who had brought the atomic bomb. This Great Flood of the present age is a kind of Universal Deluge which, instead of receding, has become frozen; and we cannot foretell when it will thaw and flow away. To change the metaphor, the twentieth century has become afflicted with a cancer — the possession of nuclear weapons by various nations — for which there is no known cure. And the souls salvaged by the people of Hiroshima are the souls of all human beings alive today.

The immediate action taken by the doctors of Hiroshima soon after the great disaster was a brilliant and impressive performance, though one hindered by enormous difficulties. One of the research projects that they conducted, however, involved some fearsome implications. I regard the questionnaire used in this project as the most morally ominous to appear so far in postwar Japan. The questions were put in a casual, modest, and even business-like manner; even so, the questions involved, by implication, a harsh accusation.

The questionnaire (only half a sheet of paper) was distributed in 1958 by the Hiroshima City Medical Association (HCMA) to its members who were surviving A-bomb victims. The replies were compiled with the following prefatory remark: 'We respectfully express our condolences to the families of those who unfortunately died after having answered the questions.' The compiled results were printed and inserted in the 'Hiroshima A-bomb Medical Care History.'[37] The print, however, is very unclear (the editors apparently did not recognize the terrible implications of the questions). So far as I could make out (using a magnifying lens), the questions were as follows:

1.  Where were you at the time of the atomic bombing (8.15 am, August 6, 1945)?
    In military service
    At an evacuation site [ie outside Hiroshima]
    In Hiroshima City
2.  Did you participate in relief activity following the bombing? If so, please give the place and period of time of your participation.

Place:

Period:

3.   Did you receive any injury caused by the atomic bomb (eg external wound, burn, serious symptoms, etc)? If so, please specify.

4.   Please give the name(s) of any other doctor(s) who participated in postbombing relief activity.

No doubt the HCMA members receiving the questionnaire felt compelled to indicate frankly whether they fulfilled their responsibilities at that time of extensive, urgent need. If there were any doctors who, though exposed to the bomb, were not directly hurt yet fled Hiroshima and did not take an active part in relief of the victims, they must have felt, when they received this questionnaire, as if they had been stabbed by a sharp knife. If the awesome impact of the bombing had robbed any Hiroshima doctor of all desire to engage in rescue work, it would not have been, humanly speaking, particularly abnormal. But after receiving the questionnaire, such a doctor could hardly have slept soundly.

In any case, the questionnaire was distributed, and the doctors responded frankly. Let me quote some sample answers (the parenthetical note gives the respondent's address and distance from the hypocenter at bombing time).

*Nobuo Satake*, deceased (Fujimicho 2-chome; 1.1 km). Was at Fujimicho 2-chome at bombing time. Received an external wound on the head. Because he had practised part-time for years, he continued to give medical treatment from that day as necessary for the relief of personnel in the clothing depot. But, on September 7, his wife died with radiation symptoms; and from about September 10, he also developed multiple radiation symptoms (eg loss of hair, subcutaneous hemorrhage, fever), and was compelled to cease giving emergency aid. His radiation symptoms continued for about three weeks afterward.

*Takeharu Tsuchiya,* deceased (Sendamachi 1-chome; 1.5 km). Was at home at bombing time. Suffered slight head lacerations. As there were injured persons in his family, he went with his family to a private house near the armory; but he was forced to go to the armory and engage in aid there, with the late Hideo Yuki and others, until the end of the war. He was then sent to Hesaka village and till October served in a first-aid station set up there by Hiroshima City.

*Sadaji Yonezawa* (Funairi Honmachi; 1.4 km). Was at Funairi Honmachi at bombing time. Suffered cuts on the back of both hands, on the chest, and on the legs. From August 6 to August 8 he took charge of first aid in Funairi Public School, along with another doctor, Hideo Furusawa. (Ten days after joining the first-aid unit, he died with radiation symptoms.)

*Kunitami Kunitomo,* deceased (Hakushima-kukencho; 1.7 km). Was at home at bombing time. Was buried under his house (the entire house and all furnishings were burned) but crawled out and escaped to the riverside behind his home, where he spent the night. From the following day (August 7), still wearing a bloody shirt, he engaged in aid to injured victims in the first-aid station at Kanda Bridge. About four months later, he moved to Etajima [an island in Hiroshima Bay]. Besides his initial injuries, other symptoms subsequently appeared: general fatigue, loss of appetite, loss of hair, and intense itching all over the body. From spring in 1948, reddish-purple eczema and skin ulcers appeared all over his body; these symptoms were treated variously. He finally died with radiation symptoms in March 1949. (Information supplied by his family.)

As is clear from these examples, the doctors in Hiroshima joined in medical relief at once, despite their own injuries. The doctors themselves, like the patients who suffered in their arms, did not know the true cause of the shocking symptoms and the terrible pain; they shared the same strong anxiety with their patients. What it was like at the relief sites can be imagined from the following excerpt from the memoirs of Dr Yoshimasa Matsusaka, then a senior member of the Hiroshima Prefecture Medical Association.

I had barely escaped death, but thought that I must try to take care of the helplessly injured citizens. As I could not walk, I had my son (a medical student at the time) carry me on his back to the East Police Station and bring out a chair from the station for me to sit on. Then he fixed the rising-sun flag to a pole at our impromptu relief site. We then began activity with the cooperation of my three nurses and of those in the neighborhood capable of helping. (When taking refuge from the bombed area, my family had packed a suitcase with a volunteer guard uniform, a fire helmet, a watch, two thousand yen, a pair of *tabi* [split-toe Japanese socks], and a rising-sun flag; these items were immediately useful.)

Although it was called medical aid, all of the stored medical supplies had been burned. In the police station there was only a little oil and mercurochrome, so of necessity I could only apply the oil to the burns and the mercurochrome to the open wounds of the many injured people who gathered there. To help revive the unconscious, we used some whiskey which I got from the police chief, Mr Tanabe. I realized that the main thing I could do was to encourage the injured patients, and having a doctor on hand was surely a psychological stimulant for the casualties. While eagerly awaiting the coming of a relief team, I used up all the oil from the police station on the many burns and wounds.

According to the 'Hiroshima A-bomb Medical Care History,' there were 298 doctors in the city of Hiroshima at the time of the bombing. All doctors were forbidden by the Air Defense Rescue Ordinance (1943) to evacuate to places outside the city. This ordinance applied to dentists, pharmacists, nurses, midwives, and public health nurses as well. That is, they were forced to stay in the city; but after the bombing, they willingly devoted themselves to relief activity. Could it be that those who sent the questionnaire to surviving doctors did not need to worry about whether the questions were too blunt or insensitive because the senders, too, had taken an active part in relief work and knew about — because they had personally witnessed — the devoted relief activities of their fellow doctors?

Sixty of the Hiroshima doctors were killed instantly by the atomic bomb. Among surviving medical personnel, 28 doctors, 20 dentists, 28 pharmacists, and 130 nurses were able to undertake relief work in a healthy condition; and as indicated by the questionnaire samples, many doctors engaged in emergency efforts despite their own serious injuries. The numbers needing treatment, however, soon swelled to more than one hundred thousand in the city alone [and over a hundred thousand more had taken refuge outside the city]. If medical personnel ever had reason to become exhausted and fall completely into despair, the handful of doctors and their colleagues trying to cope with massive need in desolated Hiroshima were such a group. In fact, one young dentist did commit suicide in despair. He had joined in the rescue work even though he had suffered fractures in both hands and burns on half his body. After overworking himself, he suffered a 'nervous breakdown'. Was this not a quite normal condition, given his experience and exhaustion? He had asked an older doctor why the people of Hiroshima still had to suffer so much even after the war had ended — and, of course, there was no adequate reply to such a question. Thirty minutes after the discussion ended, the young dentist strung a rope from a bolt jutting out from a broken wall and hanged himself. He realized that not only were people suffering now that the war had ended but also that they would continue to suffer for many years to come. A different kind of tragic battle was just beginning and would go on affecting later generations for decades. It was too much; in despair he killed himself. This young man's imagination was extremely human; but the strain of what he foresaw was more than he could bear. Only when we appreciate the tragic but by no means unnatural fate of this young dentist can we fully appreciate the remarkable efforts of the Hiroshima doctors 'who did not commit suicide in spite of everything.' A handful of doctors, some of them injured and all surrounded by a city full of casualties, had the brute courage to care for over a hundred thousand injured people with only oil and mercurochrome. The very recklessness of the doctors' courage was the first sign of hope in Hiroshima following the Great Flood of atomic destruction.

Twentieth-century literature has dealt with a variety of extreme situations, most of which are concerned with the evil found in man or in the universe. If the word 'evil' sounds too moralistic, it may be replaced with 'absurdity'. But in the various extreme situations — wars, storms, floods, pestilence — there is usually some sign of hope and recovery. These signs are found not in the fearful crisis dimensions of extremity but, rather, in the human goodwill and in the order and meaning that appear implicitly in the faint light of everyday life. A plague that ravages a city in North Africa, for example, appears as an abnormal phenomenon; but the doctors and citizens who struggle against it rely on their normal everyday human traits such as mechanical repetition, routine habits, and even patient endurance of tedium.

If a person is so clear-eyed as to see a crisis in its totality, he cannot avoid falling into despair. Only the person with duller vision, who sees a crisis as part of ongoing life, can possibly cope with it. It is precisely the 'dullness', the restricted vision, that permits one to act with reckless human courage in the face of crisis, without succumbing to despair. The lesser vision is backed by patience and, in fact, is capable of penetrating insight into the nature of a crisis.

Immediately after the atomic bombing in Hiroshima, it

is recorded, a certain prophetic voice said that no grass would grow in Hiroshima's soil for seventy-five years. Was it the voice of a foolish prophet who made a hasty mistake? Hardly. It was the voice of one making a forthright observation of a crisis situation. The prophecy soon proved false when late summer rains washed the wasted land and urged it to new growth. But was not the true damage done at a deeper level? I remember the strong, physical nausea I felt when, through a microscope, I saw the magnified leaf cells of a specimen of *Veronica persica Poir*,[38] the cells were slightly crooked in an unspeakably ugly way. I wonder whether all plants that now grow green in Hiroshima may not have received the same fatal damage.

There is no way of keeping one's balance in daily life and not be overwhelmed by crises except to believe in the green grass if it sprouts from the scorched earth before our very eyes, and thus not indulge in desperate imaginings so long as nothing abnormal happens. This is the only truly human way of living in Hiroshima. No one would continue indefinitely to make one effort after another if there were absolutely no hope for several decades that the grass would grow green again; but human beings cannot help hoping, at least for a while, that the grass will grow.

It takes a person of great care and insight to watch for any abnormality in the green grass even while it grows abundantly and healthily. A person, that is, who is humanist in the truest sense — neither too wildly desperate nor too vainly hopeful. Such genuine humanists were definitely needed in Hiroshima in the summer of 1945. Fortunately, there were such people in Hiroshima at the time; and they were the first cause for hope of survival in the midst of the most desolate wasteland of human experience.

When the young dentist agonized, 'Why must the Hiro-shima people suffer even after the war's end?' (and thereby marked the onset of another cruel battle), the older doc-tor remained silent. Even if the young man had shouted his question loud enough to be heard around the world, none of us could have answered him. His query merely voiced an absurdity for which no one has the answer. So, the old doctor kept quiet. He was busy with relief work and, naturally, overworked. Thirty minutes later the young man hanged himself, perhaps because he realized that the old doctor's silence was not just that of one individual, but of all human beings. No one could have prevented so desperate a man, with so absurd a question, from commit-ting suicide. Hence, he hanged himself. The old doctor survived and continued his relief work, and he became known as the doctor with dull but daring eyes, a man who never succumbed to despair.

That is not to say that the old doctor never uttered a word of despair in his heart. He may well have been seized with a sense of despair heavier than the young man's; but he did not surrender to it. Indeed, he had neither the freedom to surrender nor the time for suicide. With what a bitter, grief-stricken heart he took down the lifeless body of the young dentist from the broken wall — the corpse of his young co-worker whose fatal affliction was mental, not physical, despite his fractured hands and half-burnt body. Each evening the bodies of the dead were piled up in the hospital yard and burned. Perhaps the old man himself had to put the young man's body on the great heap of corpses. Surely an absurd question still lingered in his bitter, heavy heart: 'Why did the Hiroshima people still suffer so, even after the war had ended?' Yet, for twenty years he never surrendered; he simply could not.

The old doctor, Fumio Shigeto, could have been overwhelmed by a despair far heavier than that of the young dentist, for he came to know concretely and increasingly what the young man had felt and vaguely feared.

Dr Shigeto had arrived at the Hiroshima Red Cross Hospital just a week before the atomic disaster occurred. But that unprecedented event linked him to Hiroshima for life and made him a genuine Hiroshima man. Following the explosion, the first thing the doctor did, after getting back on his feet with a bloody head at the east entrance of Hiroshima Railroad Station, was to run through the utterly destroyed and still flaming streets to the Red Cross Hospital, closer than the railroad station to the central bombed area. At first, complete silence hovered over everything there. Then, suddenly, fierce cries filled the city, and these cries never ceased during the rescue activity of the doctor and his colleagues at the Red Cross Hospital. Soon the dead bodies piled up in the hospital yard began to emit a relentless foul odor.

### Give Me Water

Give me water!
  Oh! Give me water to drink!
Let me have some!
  I want rather to die —
To die!
  Oh!
Help me, oh, help me!
  Water!
    A bit of water!
I beg you!

Won't anyone?
   Oh — Oh — Oh — Oh!
   Oh — Oh — Oh — Oh!
The heaven split;
   The streets are gone;
The river,
   The river flowing on!
   Oh — Oh — Oh — Oh!
   Oh — Oh — Oh — Oh!
Night!
   Night coming on
To these eyes parched and sore;
   To these lips inflamed.
Ah! The moaning of a man,
   Of a man
     Reeling,
Whose face is
   Scorched, smarting;
     The ruined face of man!

TAMIKI HARA

Source: *Give Me Water — Testimonies of Hiroshima and Nagasaki*, edited by A Citizens' Group to Convey Testimonies of Hiroshima and Nagasaki, 1972.

While persevering in rescue work, Dr Shigeto approached the moment of awesome reality when the nature of the overwhelming, grotesque explosion would be revealed to him. Many others in Hiroshima were on the threshold of the same critical moment. A medical scholar who from his days as an unpaid junior assistant in Kyushu Imperial University's department of internal medicine had been interested in radiology, he discovered that hermetically sealed X-ray film stored in the Red Cross Hospital had been exposed [by radiation] and that camera film with which he had tried to photograph the A-bomb victims' injuries had likewise been rendered useless. When investigating the city streets, he picked up tiles on which the outline of a shepherd's purse [herb] had been imprinted. In his mind, the horrifying truth about the bomb's radioactivity began to take shape clearly. Three weeks later atomic scientists from Tokyo confirmed the nature of the bomb — an atomic bomb made with uranium (U-235).[39]

Confirmation of the bomb's nature, however, by no means resolved the immense difficulty facing the doctors: how to treat the various radiation injuries. The atomic scientists merely confirmed for Dr Shigeto and others that the 'enemy' they struggled with was the worst and strongest ever encountered. And all they had to treat the massive, complex injuries with were surgical instruments and injections of camphor and vitamins.

How did the doctors cope with what they increasingly recognized as acute radiation symptoms? Dr Tsurayuki Asakawa, chief of internal medicine in Hiroshima Red Cross Hospital at the time, speaks very frankly about this predicament, as recorded in the 'Hiroshima A-bomb Medical Care History':

People with no discernible injuries came and said that they felt listless, though they did not know why. In time, they developed nosebleed, bloody stools, and subcutaneous hemorrhages; then they would die. At first, we did not know the cause of death. As it was common sense when an illness is not clearly diagnosed to check the patient's blood, I went to the hospital basement to fetch blood analysis equipment; and when I examined the blood cells, I was astonished. It was, I realized, only natural that the patients had died, for their white cell counts were extremely low. They could not possibly have lived.

I am impressed by this physician's 'common sense', by his perseverance in a crisis situation. There was, however, no medicine available to treat what he discovered. For nosebleed, he could only insert a pressure tampon into the nose; the doctor did not know clearly the cause of the nosebleed. By the time the bleeding began, the A-bomb victims were already on the verge of death.

By the winter following the atomic bombing, most of the patients with acute radiation symptoms had died; and, at least outwardly, the critical stage of radiation illness had passed. In the struggle against the worst-ever attack on human life, mankind was defeated before the battle had hardly begun. The doctors faced such severe handicaps that they were in a losing position from the outset. Even so, Dr Shigeto and his colleagues never surrendered. They simply could not, for leukemia — the most dreadful aspect of the enemy — was beginning to rear its ugly head.

Although the enemy's overwhelming power became unmistakably clearer, the doctors did not surrender. More precisely, they simply refused to surrender. There was nothing whatsoever in the situation that encouraged them not to give up; they simply refused to do so.

If they had surrendered, the 'Hiroshima A-bomb Medical Care History' would have concluded with an account of defeat after the first few pages. Neither did the occupation forces that came into Hiroshima soon after the bombing know how to cope with the enormous monster they themselves had released. They sought clues by setting up the Atomic Bomb Casualty Commission atop Hijiyama hill and by undertaking medical examinations. But treatment of the stricken people depended entirely upon the human efforts of the surviving doctors in the A-bomb-assaulted city. And the doctors never surrendered, even though enveloped by darkness more real and urgent than that which drove the young dentist to suicide. For two decades they could not, they simply would not, give up. The atomic monster increasingly exhibited its painful, ominous powers — always superior to the strength of the doctors. But Dr Shigeto and his colleagues stood fast.

Even now there is no evidence that the human goodness which served the hapless victims has gained the upper hand over the human evil which produced the atomic bombs. People who believe, however, that in this world human order and harmony eventually recover from extremity, will perhaps take courage from the twenty-year struggle of the Hiroshima doctors — even though it cannot yet be said that they have won their battle.

# CHAPTER SIX:
# AN AUTHENTIC MAN
## December 1964

**A** traveler visits a city and gets involved in a difficult situation, but takes things into his own hands and struggles to resolve the situation. This is a formula that popular novelists often adopt. When Fumio Shigeto came to Hiroshima to become director of the Red Cross Hospital, he was like a traveler in this sense. He experienced that fatal day of the bombing before he had even become acquainted with the city's layout. A city where some pestilence rages is usually placed under martial law and is completely quarantined, like an isolated island. But when Hiroshima was attacked by radiation — the plague of the modern age — the city was not specifically closed off. Since that day, however, Dr Shigeto has, of his own volition, confined himself to this city. Immediately after the atomic bombing, Dr Shigeto, like many other doctors who aided the sufferers, began to struggle with the results of the weird new bomb. (On his way to the Red Cross Hospital right after the bombing, Dr Shigeto examined an unknown bloodied doctor and his wife at the army's East Parade Ground. The two doctors parted without learning each other's names. Afterward, in the Medical Association's questionnaire on postbombing rescue work, one doctor responded as follows: 'I was badly injured and received first aid at the East Parade Ground. But I could not help other sufferers, as I myself could not move.' So the two doctors were able to meet again after thirteen years.)

Dr Shigeto took upon himself the misery of Hiroshima, and has continued to do so for twenty years. How tenacious he has been! Yet, never in those twenty years was there one moment when the doctors could feel that they had gained complete mastery over the evil of the atomic bomb. Theirs was from the outset to now a belated, passive struggle. At times there appeared a faint gleam of hope, but each time hope was overthrown by some newly discovered symptom of misery. Dr Shigeto is, I think, typical of all the doctors of Hiroshima who have met the misery head on and have continued to struggle with it patiently. The battle, for Dr Shigeto, is not confined merely to the field of medical care; it is concerned with every difficult aspect of human society, including politics.

There are two theses in the file cabinet of Dr Shigeto's office. They are handwritten records, pursued gropingly, of early efforts to understand the nature and extent of the misery wrought by the atomic bomb. The title of the earlier thesis is 'Statistical Observations on Epilation [loss of hair] Caused by Exposure to the Atomic Bomb.' This title shows that the pursuit of understanding began with simpler, more obvious problems and proceeded step by step toward grasping the essence of atomic damage to the human body. The first observers caught a glimpse of the atomic monster's awesome form behind the statistics of the number of heads made bald by radiation.

The other thesis was written by Takuso Yamawaki, a young intern. Its title is 'On the Incidence of Leukemia among Atomic Bomb Survivors in Hiroshima and Clinical Observations on Some of These Cases.' This thesis was presented at the Japan Hematological Society in 1952 and for the first time connected leukemia with the atomic bomb, using the term 'A-bomb disease'.[40]

The doctors working directly in clinical situations were aware early on that leukemia afflicted some of the A-bomb victims in Hiroshima, and they knew that its frequency increased thereafter. Well-trained in radiology, Dr Shigeto was one of the first to make the terrible forecast about the true cause of leukemia among the Hiroshima victims. The physicians naturally made public their concern about leukemia in the newspapers, but they were severely criticized by the Atomic Bomb Casualty Commission for publicizing such dreadful prospects. Consequently, the possible connection between leukemia and atomic radiation was prevented from becoming common knowledge among the citizens of Hiroshima. Dr Shigeto then selected Yamawaki, a promising young medical scholar, and suggested that he begin compiling statistics on the actual incidence of leukemia. At the time, however, there were no statistics on the general incidence of leukemia in Japan by which one could judge whether the incidence in Hiroshima was abnormally high. Young Yamawaki, therefore, had to explore other avenues.

He wrote letters to university hospitals all over Japan in order to ascertain the instances of leukemia in each hospital. The responses gave him his first clue. For statistics on leukemia cases in Hiroshima, he examined the medical records of about thirty thousand persons in the city who had died after the war. He then called on the physician who had been in charge of each dead leukemia victim in order to confirm the diagnosis and to collect specimens.

At this point, the ABCC took note of young Yamawaki and greatly facilitated his work by making its data and a car available to him. As it was hardly common for the ABCC to be especially kind to Japanese doctors investigating A-bomb diseases in their own way, young Yamawaki's case must be regarded as particularly fortunate. Two years after he began, Yamawaki finished compiling his data and was able to stress the statistical connection between leukemia and atomic radiation.

Today Dr Yamawaki is a pediatrician in Hiroshima. His present work is not directly related to the problem of his early thesis; but when he talked to me about his work on that thesis, there was a certain yearning in his expression. I asked why he had not continued to the present time his study of leukemia among A-bomb victims. The question seemed sudden and unexpected to him, and I realized instantly that it was an improper query. We outsiders often want to find a sacrificial saint on every corner in Hiroshima. Travelers are, almost without exception, unnatural and irresponsible. Yamawaki's thesis fulfilled its mission at the right time. He went on to earn his doctorate in medicine and then build up a sound practice as a pediatrician. Meantime, Dr Shigeto has maintained an effective program of research without imposing an excessive burden on any one person.

Immediately after talking with Dr Yamawaki, I went back to the A-bomb Hospital and asked Dr Shigeto the same question, namely, whether it is generally impossible for a young scholar to continue research on A-bomb diseases after receiving a doctor's degree. Dr Shigeto's answer was as follows:

> Even for personnel of the A-bomb Hospital who study A-bomb diseases with intense passion, it is unlikely that the same disease would hold the interest of a young medical scholar throughout his career. Moreover, leukemia is a disease that cannot be cured completely; we can only treat it in standard, conventional ways. That is, it is not suitable as an object of lifelong impassioned research. To become a competent physician, it would not be advisable to concentrate exclusively on A-bomb diseases.

What a bitter, bitter taste there is to these words! It is a dread disease 'that cannot be cured completely,' so standard, conventional therapy must be repeated over and over. According to Dr Yamawaki, Dr Shigeto's sustained research on A-bomb diseases, while continuing his daily clinical work, is exceptional. Generally, it has been a taboo, especially for young doctors, to tackle A-bomb medical problems — especially if they are in hospitals that lack good research facilities. To do so was natural enough when Hiroshima was still under occupation restrictions. Under those early, more restricted circumstances, Dr Shigeto picked out a promising young intern and guided him in the development of a thesis that made a significant contribution to knowledge of A-bomb diseases; at the same time, he helped the young man to earn his doctor's degree, based on his thesis, and to establish himself in practice afterward. I think that this realistic way of doing things directly reveals Dr Shigeto's personality.

I have often heard from Dr Shigeto about the difficulties which Yamawaki encountered in pursuit of his doctorate in medicine and about Dr Shigeto's personal anxiety over it. Certainly the young intern's thesis was unusual (as soon as it was made public, it was subjected to violent attack; Dr Shigeto himself had to defend the young man from political and journalistic assaults). And it seems that his paper was not well received by the Hematological Society. This is due to the fact that the more grotesque realities of A-bomb damage were not readily apparent to ordinary human understanding.

There were some influential people who regarded the thesis as medically weak, principally because it could not explain why atomic radiation causes leukemia. The thesis rested primarily on statistics, but this alone forced recognition that there was an unmistakable increase in the frequency of leukemia among A-bomb victims in Hiroshima. Still, influential persons with fixed ideas can sometimes be obstacles to gaining such recognition.

Dr Shigeto has been responsible for the daily treatment of A-bomb patients in Hiroshima for twenty years since the atomic bombing. Before the bombing he was director of Hiroshima Red Cross Hospital, a responsibility he retained after assuming the additional post of director of the A-bomb Hospital. Since the A-bomb Hospital is not a research but a clinical facility, Dr Shigeto and his staff are on daily call to care for their patients. Any research done by them, therefore, has always had to be done in tandem with daily treatment of patients. We should remember that, by comparison, the ABCC was originally a pure research facility with no relation to clinical work.

Even so, the doctors at the A-bomb Hospital took concrete steps, while daily caring for patients, to deal with the core of the fear created by the hideous creature called the 'A-bomb' which had burrowed deeply into and was destroying human bodies. At the time, it was the only realistic option they had. The history of their efforts to cope with radiation illness is an inspiring story. They dared to work on a trial-and-error basis because they harbored the very human and natural hope of achieving positive results. Yet, in the trial-and-error approach, mistakes were sometimes made, causing some inconvenience to the patients, to citizens in general, and to the doctors themselves. It could hardly have been otherwise in Hiroshima during the past two decades.

In his two-volume work, 'The Age of Atomic and Hydrogen Bombs — Testimonies of Contemporary History,' Seiji Imahori[41] tells about the period when 'people generally felt that the dreaded atomic bomb diseases were finally under control,' as the numbers of those dying from, and those sickened by, atomic bomb diseases decreased in the winter following the bombing. In various accounts of the spread of plagues and pestilence, there are often descriptions of such a period when they slacken off temporarily. The same thing happened in Hiroshima.[42] The initial shock of the atomic plague stunned the citizens; then there was a respite that gave rise to hope. But this was followed by a second shock even more devastating to the citizens' spirits.

In the autumn of 1945, the occupation's team for investigating A-bomb damages announced that all people expected to die from radiation effects of the atomic bomb had by then already died; accordingly, no further cases of physiological effects due to residual radiation would be acknowledged.[43] This announcement was strongly oriented to political purposes, but the responses of citizens, doctors, and journalists were, as author Imahori points out, the very natural human attitudes of people at a time of momentary calm in the spread of a plague.

The decline in the number of patients in the hospitals prompted the GHQ to relax. But the decrease was related to another factor: though they were called hospitals, the glass panes had been blown out of all windows and doors. The A-bomb patients could not stand the winter cold and had taken refuge in their homes. The doctors in the hospitals, as well, thought that the A-bomb diseases had completely run their course, and they were so relieved as to take an optimistic view. The citizens and the A-bomb victims in general welcomed the good news; and the press was eager to print the encouraging views of the doctors. The Hiroshima Hospital of the Japan Medical Service system spread the news as follows: 'Among the 306,000 A-bomb survivors, patients under treatment were down to 300 in November, and now number 200. Moreover, most of these were not injured directly by radiation; rather, they have complications arising from burns and other injuries; and, because early first aid treatment was neglected, they have taken a turn for the worse. Consequently, it is safe to say that there are almost no so-called A-bomb patients' (*Mainichi Shimbun* [daily newspaper], February 6, 1946). The obstetrics and gynecology department of the Hiroshima Red Cross Hospital issued so optimistic an opinion as to imply praise of the atomic bomb: 'Recently

A-bomb victims have come, but they are all psychologically disturbed by morbid fear. A number of pregnant women have appeared from places more than one kilometer from the hypocenter, but they have no menstrual irregularities. In suburban areas three kilometers or more from the hypocenter, exposure to radiation is known to have had positive effects on patients with tuberculosis and stomach ulcers' (*Mainichi Shimbun*, February 16, 1946). Although the Hiroshima Communications Hospital is one of the best general hospitals, ranked with those of Japan Medical Service and of the Japanese Red Cross Society, it has always taken an optimistic view. Reports on conditions as of May 1946 say that in all cases but one, white cell counts had returned to normal; and patients with diarrhea had recovered. No women had given birth to deformed babies, nor had any suffered from sterility. So, the word in the department of obstetrics and gynecology is 'Relax!' (*Chugoku Shinbun*, May 13, 1946). Although surgeons were still busy with plastic operations on severely scarred tissues, they issued optimistic prognoses that disfigured places could be repaired satisfactorily. An even more optimistic opinion later came from Dr Michihiko Hachiya, director of Hiroshima Communications Hospital, who was quoted by the same newspaper (*Chugoku Shinbun*, August 8, 1948) to the effect that A-bomb diseases had completely disappeared a year ago. So, the problem seemed to have cleared up.

A more cautious scholar, Dr Shigeto, had concluded from the efforts of Hiroshima doctors and from Yamawaki's statistics that leukemia should be included among the A-bomb-induced diseases. But his work was not free from trial and error. I have already mentioned that when the atomic bomb was statistically connected with leukemia among the Hiroshima A-bomb victims, influential medical scholars would not readily accept the connection. Then, using the same statistical base, Dr Shigeto himself announced with joy that leukemia cases were decreasing. Soon after, however, he had to watch the statistical curve rise again. A trial-and-error approach, after all, must expect some error.

At the same time, the trial aspect of the approach was not a free flight of imagination unrelated to the actual care of patients; direct clinical work provided the solid base from which the doctors confirmed, step by step, the nature of the monster of radiation illness. On the other hand, it was their powers of imagination that enabled the doctors to discern the horrible shadow of the monster lurking behind the suffering of the patients.

What then, was the essence of that imagination? It was the ability to think that without the effects of the atomic bomb, a particular patient would be healthy; accordingly, the present illness of the patient may reasonably be attributed to the A-bomb effects. Or, it was the imaginative freedom — not trapped by fixed ideas — to realize that almost anything could happen to human bodies that were exposed to such a powerful, unprecedented explosion.

Medical scholars in Tokyo from time to time have questioned why a given symptom should be pathologically connected with the atomic bomb, and the Hiroshima doctors have not always had a satisfactory answer. Moreover, medical research may in time prove that in some cases there is in fact no such connection. Nevertheless, what has most helped so many A-bomb patients in Hiroshima was precisely the steady efforts of doctors who had the imagination to see that almost any symptom could be related to the A-bomb effects and after-effects.

This combination of free imagination and actual clinical work developed from the simple statistics on bald heads to the leukemia connection. It led ophthalmologists to the A-bomb cataract; it urged other Hiroshima doctors to new insights into cancer, as they analyzed data on deaths due to cancer. And it led still others to pursue persistently the possibilities of A-bomb diseases affecting future generations.

The total picture of the atomic bomb's effect on the human race is, of course, still far from clear. There remain many incomprehensible, abnormal, and even grotesque things that we simply do not yet understand. This is all the more reason why we still need doctors with free and flexible imaginations.

I heard, for instance, a story about a woman exposed to the atomic bomb at a place 800 meters from the hypocenter who was rescued and later bore two healthy children, and thus she had a happy life. On the morning of the bombing she had been playing with her classmates on the playground of her high school. Judging from the map of the A-bomb disaster area of Hiroshima, I believe it was Hiroshima Prefectural Girls' High School. Her friends all died, while she alone survived.

Why was she spared? We cannot know for sure. After Dr Shigeto told me this story, he added only the comment, 'I am happy for her.' That expression 'happy for her' still stirs a very warm feeling in my heart. But this happy woman, now a mother, came to Dr Shigeto nearly twenty years after the bombing because a dark shadow had been cast on her good fortune for the first time. The doctor's comment, 'I am happy for her,' is not so simple as it sounds. He knew that her peace and happiness were now exposed to danger; but he still felt joy in his bitter heart for the time — however short — that she could enjoy. Such things happen in Hiroshima.

Speaking of bitter hearts, free imagination by itself would be a truly terrible burden to the doctors of Hiroshima. The imaginative connection of leukemia with the atomic bomb confronts the doctors with a horrifying prospect, since the doctors themselves were exposed to the bomb. When the Hiroshima doctors pursue the A-bomb calamity in their imaginations, they are trying to see more deeply and more clearly the depth of the hell into which they too are caught. There is pathos in this dual concern for self and others; yet it only adds to the sincerity and the authenticity we sense in their dual role of imaginative research and concrete clinical care.

When Dr Shigeto thought of using high school students in the city as the target group for a comprehensive survey of A-bomb diseases among the second generation, he faced the serious dilemma that, though urgently needed, the survey might cast the students into deep anxiety. This dilemma will only deepen as radiation effects are further connected with fatal diseases like leukemia for which there is presently no cure.

This dilemma notwithstanding, research on the second generation definitely must be done, for the problem is different from that of aging and dying first-generation victims. It is the problem of people who have yet to live most of their lives. The scholars who first came from the United States to the ABCC were specialists in the field of genetics; the question of radiation effects on later generations, therefore, has been a topic of worldwide interest from the very beginning of the twenty-year history of A-bomb disease treatment. Attitudes toward the problem have fluctuated from consuming fear to an optimism that at one stage advised women to 'relax.' But now, after twenty years, a survey of A-bomb effects on the second generation is an urgent problem. Despite the grave human dilemma, Dr Shigeto will, I think, go ahead with the second-generation survey; and the high school students of Hiroshima will, I believe, cooperate with him out of genuine human respect. I do not think that the young people of Hiroshima are so suspicious that they would not trust the Hiroshima doctors who have seen the worst and tried to rise above it. These doctors are, as Homei Iwano once said, people with 'desperate brute courage.'

Deep down inside, the older teenagers of Hiroshima have great anxiety. (One of them became a hoodlum and used his keloid scars as a kind of weapon to threaten others; his anxiety and insecurity were so raw that he hid behind his keloids and turned them into a force to attack others.) But the Hiroshima doctors form the one group of grown-ups the teenagers will trust, because the doctors of Hiroshima share with them the same anxiety and, yet, have refused to surrender.

My most hopeful observation is that a survey of A-bomb diseases among all second-generation teenagers in Hiroshima will set them free from the alienation their anxiety causes and give them a new sense of solidarity.

I once interviewed two young men who had moved to Tokyo after the Hiroshima bombing. One of them was a small man with a disability in one foot; with other victim friends, he made clothes for export to America at a facility belonging to a mission school. He was a quiet, composed man. From the serenity in his eyes I could tell that he had his anxiety well under control; he could talk easily yet earnestly about the problems of leukemia and marriage that he and his companions faced.

The other young man was a laborer with a tough bearing. He had been engaged to a young woman in Kyoto; but one day he learned, from a premarital blood test, that his white cell count had increased suddenly, so he secretly abandoned his fiancée and went to Tokyo. His daily work was to nail together packing crates outside a harborside warehouse. After three days' work in the hot sun, he would spend the fourth day in bed, stuffing himself with vitamins and injecting himself with hematinics (for anemia) until his arms became hardened and discolored. He did not really believe that one day of lying abed as though dead, in a sea of medicine, would nullify three days of overwork. But the fourth day of rest gave him a feeling of psychological ease and stability. To earn that day of rest, however, he drove himself for three days to the point of physical exhaustion. While I cannot judge him as foolish, he obviously coped with his anxiety by playing a trick on himself. I have since heard that he quit the warehouse job and became a long-distance truck driver. He will probably go on punishing his body fanatically for the sake of his 'fourth day'.

The contrast between the two young men's lives is stark: one was stable, the other precarious; one was secure among friends, the other an insecure lone wolf. I often regret that

I failed to urge the settled seamster to invite the tough and troubled one into his group. The lonely laborer and I both knew, though, that the seamster was already fully occupied with problems of his own group.

A comprehensive survey of A-bomb diseases among all second-generation youth of Hiroshima — without distinguishing children of A-bomb victims — will help them discover common ground on which they can all stand together. On a larger scale, the white paper on A-bomb casualties and damages, proposed by editorial writer Kanai of the *Chugoku Shinbun,* can help the Japanese people discover the common ground, centered on Hiroshima, that they share. To my mind, these two efforts —the survey and the white paper — are the same in principle.

A full understanding of Dr Shigeto's two decades of activity since the war would include his political efforts to maintain and administer the A-bomb Hospital. But, even omitting that, the episodes sketched briefly in this essay are, I believe, enough to suggest a concrete image of the man who confronts the reality of Hiroshima squarely, neither too desperate nor too hopeful. It is just such a man that I call 'an authentic man of Hiroshima.'

The situation in Hiroshima during the past twenty years was so miserable and merciless that it would not have been enough if even a hundred authentic men had devoted themselves to it as Dr Shigeto has. But the point is that only such an authentic person could have persevered in the face of harsh adversity when, all along, the odds were never in his favor. I see Dr Shigeto as the archetype of the authentic man.

The prevailing view of China's successful nuclear test sees it as the high point of that country's recovery and achievement since its revolution. The nuclear bomb is China's utmost symbol of nationalism, a high mark of national pride. In one sense, I concur with this view. On the other hand, it is a matter of utmost urgency and necessity to point out that the atomic bombing of Hiroshima is a symbol of negation — a symbol that negates the achievements of all present and future nuclear powers, including China. As a negative symbol, it also has a positive significance for the Japanese people: it signifies a new sense of nationalism that has emerged from the dedicated twenty-year struggle to survive all that Hiroshima means. And for me, the best representative of that symbol and that struggle is precisely the 'authentic man of Hiroshima.'

# CHAPTER SEVEN:
# OTHER JOURNEYS TO HIROSHIMA
## January 1965

At the end of 1964 I made my shortest journey to Hiroshima since I began these essays. I spent only a few hours there; but, as on all previous visits to Hiroshima, my experience this time again forced me to engage in some serious reflection upon human misery and human dignity. From first to last, my various Hiroshima journeys have been like that. And the notes written after each visit were done, above all, for my own reflection.

As soon as I reached Hiroshima on my latest journey there, I heard from Dr Shigeto the latest news of the A-bomb Hospital: a young A-bomb victim had died of leukemia. Outside Hiroshima we are able to forget the misery in that city; and forgetting has become easier with the passing years, now twenty, since the atomic bombing. But there, in Hiroshima, misery continues to be a real problem. The core of that misery is embodied in the A-bomb Hospital. With what a dark and bitter heart Dr Shigeto witnessed the death of this young man — the latest of so many who have drowned in the river of misery.

The young man was exposed to the atomic bomb at age four. We have all seen many photographs of children who were wounded on the day of the bombing. Mrs Nobuko Konishi, one of the group of mothers who edit and publish the 'Rivers of Hiroshima' series, referred to the wounded children as 'putrified *jizo*' [*jizo*, the guardian saint of children, is represented in stone statues seen throughout Japan]. Surely our history will not often make such photographs possible. Most of those cruelly injured children with strangely quiet expressions died a few days after their pictures were taken. One child, who had narrowly survived, discovered after he reached his late teens that he had leukemia. He spent his twentieth birthday in bed at the A-bomb Hospital.

In the early stage of leukemia, the doctors can arrest the increase of white blood cells and bring about a 'summer vacation' (temporary remission) of the disease. After twenty years of desperate struggling, the A-bomb Hospital doctors have extended this 'summer vacation' — initially only a few months — to two years. If remission can be lengthened to tens of years, we shall be well on the way to overcoming leukemia. But at present, leukemia ('cancer of the blood') is still overwhelmingly superior to human therapeutic ability. The young man in the A-bomb Hospital had to face a two-year respite, knowing that death would not fail to overtake him. If a pessimist were to call the 'summer vacation' nothing more than a 'stay of execution', he would not be entirely wrong.

The young man, however, did not view his remaining two years as a time of deferred death. He saw that time, rather, as an opportunity to live bravely as a human being and as a member of society. The doctors at the A-bomb

Hospital helped him find a job, without disclosing his case history. It is not that the doctors engaged in a conspiracy. It is simply that, knowing no one would hire a leukemia patient, they were not so fastidious as to be afraid of making decisions about lesser matters. The young man's job was in a printing company. He was a good worker and was loved by his fellow workers.

It is said that a person of high rank visited the A-bomb Hospital following the young man's death and pressed the question, 'Why did you let him work without rest for two years?' The high-ranking person simply could not understand that, in order to live fully during the last two years of his life, it was better for the young man to be with his fellow workers and to work where the printing presses ran noisily, than to lie quietly in a hospital bed. Such understanding comes hard to 'persons of high rank' who are accustomed to phony life-styles that involve no daily work.

The young man tried to live a full life for two years. He was an able worker. He managed his social relations well. And his sincere attempt to live a life free of all falsity and sham paid off: he fell in love with a young girl, and they became engaged. His sweetheart, aged twenty, worked in a music shop.

Another episode reveals this young man's healthy attitudes toward life and society. A journalist of *Life* magazine visited Hiroshima to do an article on the 'new Hiroshima' and was introduced to this young man by Dr Shigeto. The reporter was quite satisfied with him, perhaps because the young man was the very personification of the 'new Hiroshima'.

After two years, the full 'summer vacation' came to an end. The young man suffered persistent nausea and had to return to the A-bomb Hospital. He died after enduring violent nausea and terrible pain in every joint.

A week later, the dead man's fiancée visited the A-bomb Hospital to thank the doctors and nurses who had cared for the young man. She brought a pair of ceramic deer, the kind often displayed in music stores, as a gift to the hospital. Then, with a calm and composed goodbye, she left. The next morning, the twenty-year-old girl was found dead from an overdose of sleeping pills. When I was shown the pair of ornamental deer, a strong buck with large antlers and a lovely doe, I was too sad to say anything.

Only a child of four when exposed to the atomic bomb, the youngster had no responsibility for the war, nor could he have possibly comprehended the sudden, vicious atomic attack. Yet, twenty years later, he bore the nation's responsibility in his own body. Even as a child of four he was a citizen of his country; thus, he was embroiled in the tragic consequences of his country's worst decisions. Being a member of a nation can sometimes be a sad thing.

His fiancée, however, was a child of the postwar era of peace. Yet she chose, of her own volition, to share the destiny of this young A-bomb victim; and when death took him, she tried to assume full responsibility for him by taking her own life. The nation could do nothing for him; certainly it could not redeem the full measure of his despair. But a true postwar girl tried to do so, by committing suicide. The sad and sublime voluntary choice of this young girl can only shock everyone living in this country now. It was the desperate choice of a young girl seeking to redeem the life of a young man driven into a fatal corner.

By her action, this young girl overturned the false values of the nation — specifically, the betrayal of the powerless persons who were sacrificed by the nation itself. She struck an ultimate blow against the nation and, indeed, all surviving human beings by turning her back on all their treachery and by leaving quietly to join her lover in the land of the dead, that land of lovely but harsh death which shows no mercy to anyone. She honored his death with the dignity of her own, choosing a death so completely individual as to exclude all trace of the nation that made her lover vulnerable when but a child to atomic attack and in adulthood to fatal illness. The young man's stoic diligence at work during his 'summer vacation', and the girl's brave resolution to abandon life after his death — both were clear rejections of a deceptive nation and of the surviving people. Remembering their high resolve, we cannot escape being saddened by the pair of ornamental deer, a stout buck and a lovely doe. The twenty-year-old girl, who left many gentle memories in the hearts of various people, gave her all for the young man sacrificed by the atomic bomb. She did not think of it as self-sacrifice; she acted out of the compelling love she felt for him. Her feelings could have been turned into bitter denunciation of us, the survivors, and of our political values and system. But the young girl left in silence, without recrimination, as if to dismiss all charges against the world. There was no need for us to plead extenuating circumstances. She was too gentle and dignified to level an indictment against us.

I have a hunch about the death of these two lovers. It may be only fantasy, but I believe it. The hunch is that the young man would not have wanted to go to work and live fully merely because he had two years of remission. He knew that he had leukemia, even if the doctors tried to keep it secret from others; but he was determined to live by honest labor until death from leukemia ended it all.

Moreover, I believe the young girl who fell in love with him, and became engaged to him, did so after becoming aware of his condition. In our society, an engagement between a man of twenty-four and a woman of twenty is a bit early. Knowing that his days were numbered, they decided, I feel, on an immediate engagement.

When death at last took the young man, she chose calmly and freely to follow. Her choice was not made in excessive sorrow over his death, nor out of despair over being driven into a corner where she had no other choice. She knew from the moment she fell in love with him that she must face death squarely. She chose to share his fate, and did so completely.

The American captain who piloted the weather observation plane that flew ahead of the B-29 carrying the atomic bomb, as is well known, was arrested twelve years later for raiding two post offices in Texas. He was found 'not guilty by reason of mental derangement.' A psychiatrist of the U.S. Veterans Administration testified that his mental disorder was rooted in a sense of guilt toward Hiroshima. Even for attacking official agencies such as post offices, the jury could not find the ex-captain guilty. At least, they hesitated — as would all mankind, for mankind in general has a common sense of guilt toward Hiroshima.

We all, however, need to confront the full and frightening question of guilt in a nakedly honest way. Suppose a brutal murderer appears and is apprehended, and we learn that he was led to commit heinous crimes out of despair over being bombed in Hiroshima. Who on earth would have the courage to look the criminal squarely in the eye? It is simply our good fortune that we have not had such criminals appear to force the question of our own guilt. And we should acknowledge gratefully that this good fortune results from the surprising spirit of self-restraint of the Hiroshima people who had every reason to fall into such despair.

It is enough to jolt our nonchalant attitude simply to imagine that the resolute young man who died of leukemia had become a criminal instead of a steady, hard worker in his last two years. He worked stoically and found a sweetheart so devoted that she followed him quietly to death. Their behavior represents a very rare achievement, far surpassing ordinary sensibilities. Their situation was exceedingly bitter and desperate; had they fallen into immorality, madness, or crime, we could only regard it as quite human. But they did not succumb to such temptations. Instead, they lived stoically and with dignity to the end, despite all, and then passed quietly through death's door.

Often I wonder if the American military leaders responsible for the decision to drop the atomic bomb did not perhaps take too lightly the consequent calamity. I wonder if they did not depend too much upon the ability of Hiroshima's citizens to recover, and upon their sense of honor and independence to prevent them from stagnating in their misery. All of us should remember that we have been able to retain fairly clear consciences thanks solely to the remarkable spirit of self-restraint of the A-bomb victims who never surrendered to despair.

An easygoing conscience, however, cannot remain untroubled except by intentionally refusing to listen to the stories that come out of Hiroshima. Here I must record two such stories that came to my attention after my latest journey to Hiroshima. One comes from a column in the *Yomiuri Shinbun* (January 19, 1965; evening edition).

A nineteen-year old girl in Hiroshima committed suicide after leaving a note: 'I caused you too much trouble, so I will die as I planned before.' She had been exposed to the atomic bomb while yet in her mother's womb nineteen years ago. Her mother died three years after the bombing. The daughter suffered from radiation illness; her liver and eyes were affected from infancy. Moreover, her father left home after the mother died. At present there remain a grandmother, age seventy-five; an elder sister, age twenty-two; and a younger sister, age sixteen. The four women had eked out a living with their own hands. The three sisters were all forced to go to work when they completed junior high school. This girl had no time to get adequate treatment, although she had an A-bomb victim's health book.

As a certified A-bomb victim, she was eligible for certain medical allowances; but the [A-bomb victims medical care] system provided no assistance with living expenses so that she could seek adequate care without excessive worry about making ends meet. This is a blind spot in present policies for aiding A-bomb victims. Burdened with pain and poverty, her young life had become too exhausted for her to go on. . . .

There is something beyond human expression in her words 'I will die as I planned before.'

The other story comes from the Chikuho coal fields in

northern Kyushu. Economically depressed, [44] the Chikuho district represents the low point of our prosperous consumer society, the dark side of all social and political distortions. It is said that many people migrated to this district from Hiroshima, as though driven away. Among them were women who lost their families in the atomic bombing and who are now engaged in the lowest occupations. There must be some Hiroshima women in the Chikuho district who will never reveal their identities, no matter how effectively the nationwide survey for the A-bomb white paper is conducted.

Those of us outside Hiroshima are stirred to a new awareness by stories like these, as if strong acid were poured into our eyes and ears; but soon we turn our attention to other things. I am afraid there are people like us even among the non-victims in Hiroshima.

In this connection, it is worth noting that, at the same time that the young leukemia victim died and his fiancée killed herself, a ceremony was held to confer the First Class Order of the Rising Sun (Kun'itto Kyokujitsu Daijusho) on General Curtis E. LeMay, then U.S. Air Force Chief of Staff. This same general was one of those who had participated in planning the military operations for dropping the atomic bombs on Hiroshima and Nagasaki. It is reported that an official representing the Japanese government said: 'I, too, had my house burned down in an air raid; but that was twenty years ago. Is it not magnanimous, as befits a great nation, to go beyond love and hate and give a decoration to a military man who bombed Japan's cities during the war?'

This kind of insensitivity shows how far moral breakdown has already gone in our country. Had this scene been witnessed by the people of Hiroshima, they would have seen it as a betrayal of their suffering, of their devastated city, and of their disfigured bodies and lives. We are much too tolerant of the moral aberrations of statesmen and bureaucrats. Unless they commit some gross and vulgar immorality, the press does not attack their moral depravity. But a statesman who utters such words as those quoted above represents immorality of the worst sort.

While in Hiroshima, I interviewed four of the most representative people of the city for a television program. They were Dr Fumio Shigeto, director of the A-bomb Hospital; Mr Toshihiro Kanai, editorial writer for the *Chugoku Shinbun*; Mrs Nobuko Konishi, one of the editors of the 'Rivers of Hiroshima' series; and Miss Yoshiko Murato, a young A-bomb victim who works as an office clerk in a private hospital in Hiroshima. These four were interviewed together in a panel discussion held in a room next to the data showroom at the A-bomb Hospital.

Except for Miss Murato, I had often met these persons. One aim of this note is to introduce how these people live and what they think. Some of the TV footage was devoted to indicating the latest developments in their work. I was pleased to participate in this discussion; and I am particularly gratified to record the interview with Miss Murato, another typical unsurrendered A-bomb victim.

Only a small child when she experienced the atomic bombing, Miss Murato's face was disfigured by keloid scars. After she grew up, her daily hope was to see her former undamaged face; or, in her own words, to recover her 'lost beauty'. She underwent a number of operations not for her health but for the restoration of her features, only to learn that she could never recover her 'lost beauty'. Following the operations, she realized that she would have to live as did numerous girls with keloids; so she retired quietly to the back rooms of her home in Hiroshima.

Dwelling on the lost past and the attendant despair can push a person into deep neurosis. There must be many Hiroshima people in such a critical state. I do not claim that we have any effective means of saving these people from madness or suicide. We can only hope that, despite their misery, they can manage to go on living without succumbing to such extremes.

What kept Miss Murato from committing suicide at the point of madness or despair? What prevented her from spending her life as a secluded hermit? Her conversion was precipitated by the First World Conference against Atomic and Hydrogen Bombs (1955), where she discovered the basic and crucial fact that she was 'not the only person who suffered.'[45] After the long, dark, and silent days of intense, isolated, individual suffering, the First World Conference gave the people in Hiroshima their first chance to speak out, and with each other. How often I heard them refer to it as 'an epoch-making event.' That conference not only gave direction to the peace movement in Japan and in the world; it also gave the A-bomb victims an opportunity to regain their humanity. It is difficult for an outsider such as myself to assess the peace movement objectively. But it is a fact that the First World Conference against A- and H-bombs occasioned a human revolution among the A-bomb victims, although the movement and subsequent world conferences gradually changed in nature. It is not a groundless criticism to say that in the changes a certain degeneration can be discerned. Needless to say, the degeneration did not stem from the side of the A-bomb victims.

Grasping the opportunity afforded by the First World Conference, Miss Murato recovered from the neurotic condition which had made her turn toward the past and live in absolute privacy; she became capable of dealing with the present and the future. She participated in the A-bomb victims' peace movement, traveled to foreign countries, and in France met Mme. Irène Joliot-Curie (1897-1956),[46] who was to die shortly from leukemia. Mme Joliot-Curie said that she could understand all the suffering of Miss Murato and the other 'A-bomb maidens', however silent they remain. Those who are called A-bomb maidens must have the same kind of conversion as Miss Murato, she continued, to surmount the yearning for 'lost beauty' and the hatred and shyness caused by the keloids that distort their faces. The disfigured young girls who endured the hot sun as they stood on the platform at the world conference, we must realize, were persons who had experienced a conversion that made it possible for them to admit openly their condition. Dr Shigeto and Miss Murato spoke of the peace movement participants' wish that 'other people not be made to taste the same suffering' as had the A-bomb maidens and other A-bomb victims. Clearly, the A-bomb maidens and Mme Joliot-Curie understood each other completely.

On the day of the TV panel discussion, Miss Murato hesitated to the last moment to talk for public broadcasting. Her conversion was not settled once and for all, like a creed; it had to be kept alive by being renewed each day. The young woman's refreshing face overflowed with beautiful resolve and thus must have impressed the TV audience. She spoke on behalf of all young women in Hiroshima who are marred by keloid scars. When these sufferers shoulder their burdens with such dignity and struggle openly against the A-bomb misery, the Hiroshima doctors can doubtless do their work more effectively.

The brief span of a TV program was not adequate, of course, for a full explanation of the white paper plan of Mr Kanai. He therefore put the plan in the context of his own views of man and civilization, of perspectives that have grown out of his twenty-year career as a journalist in Hiroshima. Indeed, it would have been impossible to explain the plan apart from these perspectives.

Two points in Mr Kanai's way of thinking became clearer to me in the process of making the TV film. One is that, while the realities of the Auschwitz holocaust perpetrated by Nazi Germany against the Jews is well known around the world, the Hiroshima experience is not so well or widely known, even though the scope of misery caused in Hiroshima far exceeds that of Auschwitz. Besides, there is a very real danger that the Hiroshima-type disaster may occur again (cynics might say that, if so, it will be for an Auschwitz-type purpose!). In any case, the reality of human misery in Hiroshima must be made as well and widely known all over the world as is that of Auschwitz.

The other point is rooted in Mr Kanai's view of civilization. If we think of the misery of war as being at the center of human affairs, the Japanese people have since Hiroshima been fleeing in all directions away from the center. Thus, we have developed a 'doughnut' view of life, keeping as much distance as possible from war's misery at the center. With the growth of our affluent consumer society, our standard of living has risen dramatically; so, to add a vertical dimension to this perspective, we leave the tragedy of war at the very bottom and seek to rise higher and higher above it. With our double effort to get away from, and also above, the misery of war, the simple doughnut has been replaced by a three-dimensional pyramid as the shape of our common lifestyle — with the Olympics at the top. The deep, dark cavern inside the pyramid, however, has never been filled. The human misery of Hiroshima continues to exist there. The campaign for a white paper on the A-bomb damages and casualties is one important way to make the human misery of Hiroshima thoroughly and accurately known to the whole world, as is Auschwitz's. The Japanese people, as a vital part of their evaluation of their own history and morality, must accept the duty of filling the empty cavern within the pyramid of their affluent consumer society. Unless we perform this duty, we shall not be able to prevent desperate people from committing suicide as their way of asserting there is no longer any hope or salvation — as happened in the case of the nineteen-year-old girl who ended her life 'as planned before.'

Ever since I heard of Mr Kanai's white paper proposal last summer, I have tried to follow this campaign closely. It appears to be proceeding steadily, at least as concerns the efforts of Mr Kanai and his colleagues. Soon after I introduced the white paper plan in an earlier essay, I received a letter from Mr Kanai, early last autumn. His letter clearly reveals his attitude on attending the Three-Prefecture Liaison Conference last summer.

Not only at this conference but also at the peace rally on August sixth, the people who have the right to speak most boldly and plainly about the realities of the A-bomb victims are the victims themselves, and especially the dead victims. One minute of silent prayer in their honor had just that meaning. . . .

As a journalist, Mr Kanai wants to convey clearly the moans of the surviving sufferers and the voiceless voices of the dead victims.

The most difficult problem in trying to produce a white paper on A-bomb casualties and damages is how to deal with the conservative government. Basically, it may be a problem of how to extract a purified bravery from our soiled national flag. A number of professors at Hiroshima University have organized the Peace Problems Research Group; it is one of the few forums where some of the representatives of the three separate conferences[47] held this summer can and do meet each other on good terms. At a recent meeting of this group, I reported once again on the proposal to compile a white paper for presentation to the United Nations. As a result, a small committee was formed to work out a concrete plan.

While this project must maintain its strong grounding in the basic understanding of the A-bomb victims themselves, the practical question is how much of a nationwide base we need and can hope to build, apart from the conservative government and the mass media. This includes the need to appeal to the Science Council of Japan and to the various government ministries of Health and Welfare, Education, and Foreign Affairs — as well as to the Prime Minister's Office, with the hope of getting a bipartisan decision in the National Diet for a supplementary survey to be conducted in conjunction with the national census [scheduled in 1965]. And the problems of conducting a survey include the need to secure case-workers of the highest competence and intelligence. The problems are much too large for any one person, and I myself intend to cooperate from the sidelines, for what is needed is a twofold approach that both mobilizes the best brainpower in this country and also builds a broad national base of support. I know my own limits and intend to keep out of the way, trying only to fulfill my duty to make the conception and direction of the project as clear as possible.

The Peace Problems Research Group which approved Mr Kanai's proposal in October of last year issued two documents: 'A Request to the Government of Japan' and 'An Appeal to the People of Japan.' These two documents made clear the importance of including in the 1965 national census a supplementary survey of the conditions of victims of the atomic bombings and of hydrogen bomb tests. In this connection, the documents urged the necessity of respecting the privacy of victims as well as the need to extend the scope of the survey beyond Japan, beginning with the Ryukyu Islands.[48] Those of us outside Hiroshima also need to give this effort our full cooperation. In Mr Kanai's words, we need to stand on the side of 'the human moans of the A-bomb victims' and to become their 'comrades'.

Mrs Nobuko Konishi and her colleagues published the tenth issue of 'Rivers of Hiroshima' early this year. It is one example of how the white paper campaign is gaining momentum. The preface reads:

In Japan at present there are signs of new threats to peace. To us A-bomb victims, these signs are frightening. The politicians are eager to show off their power, while we, the common people, have nothing to show. We have only words to appeal to the truth.

Miss Shinoe Shoda, who today is bedridden with radiation illness, recently published a collection of poems under the title 'Penitence.'[49] The cover has a sketch of the A-bomb Dome and a verse that reads, 'For the souls of our countrymen/who were forced to die/I offer a diary of sorrow.' The collection includes some poems composed in 1947 by A-bomb victims during the period when they were forced to keep silent by restrictions imposed by the occupation GHQ; these poems were among the first efforts to depict the misery caused by the atomic bomb. Poems and songs by this indomitable poet herself are also included. One of her poems severely criticizes the conferring of an order of merit on General Curtis LeMay. Two short verses have a kind of sorrowful and bitter humor that hits us right in the pit of our stomachs.

> I lost my sight in the bombing,
>    says the girl of twenty;
> but I'll gladly give my eyes to someone
>    when I die.

> 'I'll give my eyes,' I said,
>    'when I die.'
> But bomb-damaged eyes, I was told,
>    are of no use at all.

The postscript to the collection of poems takes up an earlier proposal to demolish the A-bomb Dome; and the critique given at that time relates directly to the current need for a white paper on A-bomb casualties and damages.

The problem of demolishing the A-bomb Dome has been smoldering for a long time. Some people point out that the Peace Park area has been put in order, and now the dome matter should be dealt with concretely. Land in the vicinity of the dome is valued at 200,000 yen per *tsubo* [3.3 square meters], so it would be better to erect a commercial building that would bring revenue to the city. The atomic bomb has become well known throughout the world, so it is best to tear down the dome now. It only reminds us of dead people, anyway, and so on. To those who say, 'Tear it down,' I feel like thundering, 'Nonsense!' We surviving victims have made a solemn pledge that the same terrible disaster must never be repeated, and we should retain the dome as a monument dedicated to peace for all mankind. The atomic bomb is known to all the world, but only for its power. It still is not known what hell the Hiroshima people went through, nor how they continue to suffer from radiation illnesses even today, nineteen years after the bombing. The preservation of the dome, therefore, must be considered from a worldwide point of view.[50]

Always moderate in expression, Dr Shigeto did not talk very much during the TV panel discussion. But what he did say, and his firm resolution, impressed me. He stressed the need to monitor the health of children born of A-bomb victims (being careful not to incite anxiety in those to be investigated, and also being sensitive to their right to privacy). He fully realizes that the superpowers are proud of their nuclear arms; he also knows that medical examinations of the second genereation could turn up results that, in the long run, would be a definite stain on the superpowers. He expressed his hope that Japan would be blessed with politicians who would never permit that stain to come to our country; that is, we must adhere strictly to our policy of not possessing, producing, or permitting the entry of nuclear weapons. And we must oppose their possession by other countries. I have met Dr Shigeto many times on my various journeys to Hiroshima, but this was the only time I ever heard him refer directly to political affairs.

# EPILOGUE:
# FROM HIROSHIMA
## January-May 1965

In April I wrote a letter to the Japan Confederation of A-bomb and H-bomb Sufferers Organizations (JCSO), which is planning to collect and publish data on A-bomb experiences; I wrote to request that a committee of intellectuals be formed to cooperate with the JCSO plan. The request reads as follows:

> As we approach the twentieth summer since the atomic bombing, the Japan Confederation of A-bomb and H-bomb Sufferers Organizations, the only nationwide body for A-bomb victims, is embarking upon a very necessary and important enterprise: to collect all data on the atomic bomb, including the memoirs of A-bomb victims, in order to preserve them properly. This is an urgent task — both for the victims forced to endure cruel circumstances for twenty years and also for the rest of us — whether the atomic bombs dropped two decades ago were the last ever to be used against human beings or the newest nuclear weapons should be used tomorrow to massacre people again.

The JCSO's former connection with the Japan Council against Atomic and Hydrogen Bombs undoubtedly gave it great political leverage; at the same time, the alliance was not adequate for accomplishing what the A-bomb victims themselves regarded as most urgent. The plan now being initiated independently by the JCSO clearly deals with this fundamental problem.

The compilation of data and memoirs is an undertaking that stems from the A-bomb victims' stoic self-affirmation and determination to shape their own destinies; it also offers us non-victims an opportunity for self-understanding today and for reflecting on what lies ahead tomorrow. It is my feeling, therefore, that concerned people not exposed to the atomic bomb should, out of admiration and respect for the victims, assume some cooperative role in this undertaking.

When an intelligent person reflects on his own personal destiny and on that of all mankind, he cannot avoid recalling those who experienced the atomic bombings of twenty years ago. He should think, then, of how his own aspirations are, and ought to be, linked with those of the A-bomb victims.

Concerned intellectuals who commit themselves to such efforts, however, often find that they are insulated from reality and thus sometimes lose sight of their goals before reaching them. Often it is not clear how far one should go, or whether one's expectations can be fulfilled, or even how much responsibility one has.

I therefore propose the formation of a committee of concerned intellectuals to cooperate with the JCSO plan, realizing that the intellectuals should seek to align their thought and aims with the life and aspirations of the A-bomb victims as the best way to clarify the commitments, expectations, and responsibility of those who would cooperate.

As summer 1965 approaches, a number of efforts are under way to ascertain and reassess the worst aspects of the misery that began twenty years ago. Collecting and compiling all kinds of data as well as the personal testimonies of the A-bomb victims are essential to these efforts. Journalists once made public some of the data, but most of their reports have since been lost in the endless flood of publications. The early data and memoirs, however, are both invaluable and irreplaceable, as they were composed under conditions impossible to repeat.

Many of us remember the 'A-bomb drawings'[51] by Mr Iri Maruki and Miss Toshiko Akamatsu as an excellent record of the human situation following the bombing. But how many people can recall their small book of drawings with the title 'Flash-Bang,'[52] published in 1950? This illustrated book with an orange cover, graced by a portrait of an old woman, is nothing less than shocking. I shall introduce some of the short but revealingly accurate captions here, in the hope that all of the sixty-four drawings and the explanatory sentences will be reprinted.

An eighty-year-old woman of Mitaki township in Hiroshima lost her husband in the 'flash' of the bomb; day and night she still tells her grandson Tomekichi the 'flash story', like a thread woven in childhood.

It was just like hell — a procession of ghosts, a sea of flames. But I didn't see the devil, so I thought it was something happening on this earth. . . . An atomic bomb doesn't just fall; someone has to drop it.

To this day, even after five years, the old woman tells her story incessantly, recalling details of wind and rain. She remembers, and deplores her memories: 'The war was almost over. Everyone hated it. But they were all submissive, and heeded every beck and call of the army and the government.'

On that fatal morning, an old man and an old woman had taken a drawcart to fetch some lumber from houses torn down to create firebreaks; after returning home, they were taking a bath when the bomb exploded. 'It was eight o'clock. There was a great flash; it was like nothing ever seen before. The old woman neither felt a jolt nor heard a bang. The ceiling and the roof just fell down together, the floor jumped up, and she was caught in between them.'

In the central bombed area, there were 'two feet of a victim whose body had vanished in a single puff; they stood upright, stuck to the concrete road.' Again, strangely, 'in a streetcar . . ., a young girl lay dead, head to head with a dead, charred-black soldier; uninjured but with torn clothing, she still clutched her purse.' But, 'not a soul remained to tell us what happened at the center of the bombed area.' The image evoked by these short, heartbreaking sentences is one of a darkened sky, fallen bare trees, and a desolate scorched earth.

In the pond of the Sentei [Asano Mansion], live carp were swimming among the dead bodies.

A swallow with burned wings could no longer fly; it just hopped around on the ground.

When I came to my senses, I found my comrades still standing erect and saluting; when I said, 'Hey,' and tapped their shoulders, they crumbled down into ashes.

In the home of a sick soldier, his young wife was crushed between large, heavy beams, still holding her child in her arms. A man from next door tried to rescue her, but the beams were more than one man, or even two, could lift. Wanting to save her child at least, he cried, 'Quick, give me the baby!' But she said, 'No, let us die here together. My husband is already dead, anyway. I can't leave this child alone.... Hurry up! Escape while you can.' This young mother's choice is, in a way, more touching than a self-sacrifice that leaves a baby alone in this world.

Food was distributed to the A-bomb victims. An old woman's grandchild was standing in line to receive rations. 'In front of my grandchild, there was a young near-naked girl. After receiving rations for five persons, she fell forward on the ground and lay motionless.'

At that time, flies supped on human blood; and a rumor spread that no grass or trees would grow, so people could not make a living for seventy-five years.

People who exclaimed, 'We survived,' died later with spots all over their bodies and with their hair falling out.

A mother in Mitaki township, who lost her husband in the atomic bombing, carried on her daily work valiantly; but on her arm where skin from her hip had been transplanted, the scar tissues continued to contract in autumn and winter, causing intense pain.

An old woman, whose husband had died of prostration, began to paint pictures every day. They were beautiful, bright pictures, with red flowers and pretty doves. Even today, she says, 'An atomic bomb is quite different from a landslide; one never falls unless someone drops it.'

When this small picture book was published, it attracted the attention of many people, as it was a faithful account of the A-bomb experience and had a fascinating charm. In the same summer, however, another book was scheduled for publication in Hiroshima; though printed and bound, it was suppressed by the occupation forces because it depicted too vividly the A-bomb realities, and it was anti-American as well. The year was 1950, and the Korean War had just started. It was the same year that an American reporter asked a blind A-bomb victim: 'I suppose we could end the war if we dropped two or three atomic bombs on Korea; as an A-bomb victim, what's your opinion?'

The suppressed book was buried deep in the storeroom of Hiroshima City Hall and was not discovered until this April. Now the city is planning to reissue it. It is a most appropriate book for reissue on the twentieth anniversary of the first atomic bombing. The editor of the original volume wrote, in anticipation of its publication:

This book consists of documents which tell the unblemished truth about the misery experienced in Hiroshima five years ago. Submitted contributions numbered 160, and each one moved us to tears. Considering the variety of the surroundings, the actual conditions described, and the distances from the hypocenter at bombing time, we chose eighteen contributions to print in full and sixteen excerpts which depict particular experiences. The rest of the manuscripts are to be stored in the Hiroshima Peace Memorial Hall as treasures of this city of peace.

At this time when the two hostile camps of the world are engaged in fierce battle, may these sacred compositions — by people who suffered mankind's worst disaster and have survived through great agony and sorrow — be received widely as a heaven-sent appeal for peace.

It was in fact three years after the bombing when the submitted manuscripts were written. In what frame of mind did 164 Hiroshima people want to record their miserable experiences — being forced thereby to relive them again? Their attitude is reflected in the pressing urgency of the memoirs of a professor at Hiroshima University of Literature and Science, who had been exposed to the atomic bomb at a place two kilometers from the hypocenter.

No more war! No more war! This is the cry that wells up from the bottom of the sad hearts of Hiroshima's A-bomb victims. It is a genuine plea for peace that defies adequate expression. I pray that no one will ever again suffer such a cruel experience, for whatever reason. I direct my appeal to the whole world: lift high the call, 'No more Hiroshimas!' Lift it as high as possible over the tense international situation of the world today. It should not remain confined, solitary and lonely, to the Peace Cenotaph by Otagawa River.

This passage expresses well the general feeling of the A-bomb victims at that time, three years after the bombing. That is, there should be some kind of positive guarantee that human beings would never again undergo such misery; nothing less could ultimately assuage their own misery. Moreover, in only three years' time they were already beginning to feel that their deepest wish was being trapped, 'solitary and lonely,' in the Peace Cenotaph by Otagawa River.

A third-year elementary school boy, who narrowly escaped the bombing because he was evacuated with other school children, wrote at the time about the thing that took his father's life and wounded his mother and younger brother. 'The A-bomb, the A-bomb — it is the devil that took my father's life. But I cannot bear a grudge against the atomic bomb. Because of it the people of our city rose up to insist, "No more Hiroshimas, no more Hiroshimas." The people who died can be said to have sacrificed themselves for us. Their sacrifices are invaluable, and we should walk the way of peace, watched over by those noble victims.'

This boy's thoughts reflect the efforts of public school teachers at the time, under the occupation, to justify the misery caused by the atomic bomb. It is clear, too, that he struggled with too many weighty contradictions that had been crammed into his head. However logically he tried to cope with the atomic bomb, it was something he absolutely could not accept. Still, he could write, 'I cannot bear a grudge against the atomic bomb.' That one line cuts into our hearts.

The most striking feature of these records of that terrible summer twenty years ago is the *silence* of the citizens following the bombing. The great mysterious monster conquered the city in an instant. Was it unnatural that the basic reaction of the people, injured and demoralized, was stunned silence?

A clerk at a fuel distribution control center one hundred meters from the hypocenter was the only survivor of his group, because he had gone down into the basement just before the bomb exploded. Here is his observation:

> Everyone gathered at some stone steps and sat down. They included a woman losing her sight in one eye, a man getting sicker by the minute, another with a fierce headache. Everyone had external and internal injuries, but no one cried out in pain. Almost everyone was silent.

It was a cruel and complete silence, worse than any other, like 'a moan that cannot be voiced.' One woman recorded her experience:

> I ran toward Tsurumi Bridge, jumping over stones and fallen trees as though I were mad. What did I see there? Countless people were struggling to get to the stream under the bridge. I could not distinguish men from women. Their faces were swollen and gray; their hair stood on end. Then, raising both hands skyward and making soundless groans, they all began jumping into the river as though competing with one another.

Another young woman's observation makes even clearer the character of the silence that took deep root inside the A-bomb victims; there is a more complicated psychological evolution in her account.

> The concrete wall opposite me had big, gaping holes in places. I approached it because some low, dark figures seemed to be sitting in a row at its base. I could hardly tell man from woman or child, nor could I distinguish their ages. They were all but nude, sitting in a line; and their faces and bodies had swelled up and turned brown, as if by common consent. One had already become

blind. Then I noticed a baby on someone's knee; the skin of its back was hanging down, as if a rotten, reddish loquat had been peeled off all around. Instinctively, I turned away from the sickening sight. They were all motionless and kept a strange silence. It seemed that the question of life and death was yet unsettled for them. I shuddered at the thought of being loaded on a truck with these people.

Her modest self-concern, however, lasted only a short while. Soon she lost consciousness. When, a full day later, she regained consciousness, a new realization swept over her: 'I'm blind! I tried to raise my hands, but my right hand was heavy and beyond my control. With the fingers of my left hand I touched my face lightly; my eyebrows, my cheeks, and my mouth felt like a mixture of bean curd and gelatine. My face was swollen, like a big sponge; it was as if I had no nose. I shuddered as I suddenly remembered the spooky shapes at the foot of the concrete wall.' At this point, however, she had no choice but to join the circle of gloomy silence.

Then there was born within her a sense of solidarity with all A-bomb victims in Hiroshima. Instead of withdrawing with a shudder, she accepted a common destiny with her fellow victims.

One year I heard that a medical team would come to examine A-bomb victims. So I went to the hospital and found myself among others with various A-bomb disease symptoms. A forty-year-old woman, now living far away in Miyoshi, had scars around her eyes and mouth; her face was so horribly altered by keloid scars that one could hardly look at it squarely. One side of the face of a beautiful young single woman was covered with dark reddish keloids from cheek to neck, and it seemed that she could not turn her neck freely. One man had three fingers that were stiffened and strikingly small. They all talked much about the cruelty of war and the bitter remorse of living, and they shed tears openly. I was much better off than they, but could offer no comforting words. I felt sorry for them; and the sight of them, burned into my mind, is still with me. Can nothing be done for them? Life will probably be dismal for them as long as they live.

A student who, at age seventeen, had been working at a factory in the suburbs with the Student Mobilization Corps, was on his way home soon after the bombing to search for his family in the ruined city, when the 'black rain'[53] fell. He was 'moved by the faint groans of children buried alive,' and joined in their rescue. A junior high school teacher, who had been helping to rescue pupils and clearing away dead bodies all day long, wrote the following at the end of the grueling day's work.

Beyond the dim light of cremation fires, there is nothing but dead bodies neatly piled up and, among the survivors, all the swollen faces, the tattered clothes, the groans, and the deep sleep. Two or three pupils have already been sent to first-aid stations, and the rest are to be taken to hospitals in Nijima and Miyajima. After confirming that they will receive treatment at the hospitals, and entrusting them meanwhile to the care of the rescue squad, we went to get a pupil who was to wait for us at the foot of Hirose Bridge. It was half past four. When we reached the bridge, however, we found only the dead body of an old person unknown to us. The pupil was nowhere to be found. The four of us (teachers) returned to the school in silence. Under the pre-dawn stars, we sat down back-to-back behind the remains of the charred school gate and fell into a deep sleep.

These exhausted, silent teachers knew only a bitter, bitter sleep. . . .

What is life like today for the 164 Hiroshima citizens who submitted their memoirs for the book of recorded A-bomb experiences? How many are alive and healthy? Seventeen years have passed since they wrote their memoirs. Their urgent cries — uttered to assuage the pain of their experiences, to evaluate them in their own way, and to find in them some positive meaning — have until this April been buried in the City Hall storeroom like dead books or mere wastepaper. One hundred and sixty-four A-bomb victims dared to voice their cries despite their physical pain and spiritual suffering; but the heavy hand that wielded power silenced them at once. Even the most optimistic estimate would have no grounds for believing that most of the contributors are still living. Those who had died by this April must have passed away with bitter chagrin, thinking that their once-uttered cries were sealed in silence forever. Who can adequately atone for their unfulfilled desire to be heard?

The time has come to end these notes on Hiroshima, begun after I had visited the city in the summer of 1963 and again the next summer. I once thought of exposing my own intentions more clearly in the title to the book of collected essays; I considered various possibilities, such as:

Thinking of the People in Hiroshima
The Hiroshima Within Us
How Shall We Survive Hiroshima?

For the advertising blurb for my novel 'A Personal
Matter,'[54] published last year, I wrote: 'I tried anew to
achieve some basic refinement in my thinking on several
topics of importance to me.' I have written this series of
essays on Hiroshima with the same intent; though 'Hiroshima' is, I dare say, the most difficult matter to handle at
a basic level. By taking Hiroshima as the fundamental
focus of my thought, I want to confirm that I am, above all,
a Japanese writer.

It was in the summer of 1960 that I first visited Hiroshima. Although at that time I had not yet begun to
understand Hiroshima, I had one clear intimation of it. A
short essay that I wrote for the *Chugoku Shinbun* included
this passage: 'Today I visited Hiroshima and attended the
A-bomb Memorial Ceremony. It was a precious experience for me. I still feel it is. The impact of that experience
will grow and deeply influence me. During the fifteen
years since the bombing, I passed the springtime of my
life. I should have visited Hiroshima earlier; the earlier,
the better. But it was not too late for me to visit there this
year.'

This intimation became reality. Hiroshima, has, indeed,
become the weightiest and most influential factor in my
thinking. I often dream very suffocating, painful dreams.
For instance, in a certain place at high noon in midsummer, I see a small, strained, middle-aged man in his pajamas
and robe with his head held erect like an Awa doll, and he
speaks in a scarcely audible voice. In this dream, I listen to

his voice and realize that in a few months he will die, wasted away by an A-bomb disease.

But the human tragedies I witnessed in Hiroshima — even if seen only by a traveler's eye, and though I do not have the courage to turn hopeless tragedy into something of positive value — at least made clear to me wherein lies the human dignity of the Japanese people.

In Hiroshima, I met people who refused to surrender to the worst despair or to incurable madness. I heard the story of a gentle girl, born after the war, who devoted her life to a youth caught in an irredeemably cruel destiny. And in places where no particular hope for living could be found, I heard the voices of people, sane and steady people, who moved ahead slowly but with genuine resolve. I think it was in Hiroshima that I got my first concrete insight into human authenticity; and it was there also that I saw the most unpardonable deception. But what I was able to discern, even faintly, was altogether only a small portion of an incomparably larger abominable reality still hidden in the darkness.

In the eleventh issue of 'Rivers of Hiroshima,' Miss Kimiko Okuda wrote as follows:

Hundreds of people arrived at the clinic in burnt, ragged clothes, dragging their feet. Eager to know what had happened, I asked them. They all answered, 'Houses were knocked down by the flash and bang, and people were engulfed in a great ball of flame. We don't really know what happened.' We all listened intently. To what could it be compared? Even as they talked, these people collapsed one after another. I could only think of the 'Picture of Hell.'[55]

'The Picture of Hell.' Throughout human history, people have had various nightmarish visions of the end of the world. In the latter half of the twentieth century, the image of the world's final days, once depicted in religious terms, is now portrayed by science fiction fantasies. Of all the eschatologies offered by science fiction, the most terrible is a final demise caused by the transformation of natural human blood and cells — and thus of human beings as such — into something grotesque and inhuman. The plagues and wars of medieval times must have given people a glimpse of what the end of civilization would be like. But people then could envision God behind all misfortune and thus hope that, after their death, another people would dare to till the soil and fish the seas. Eschatologies prior to the twentieth century still contained some sense of composure. People could believe that the end of the world would be experienced as having some kind of human shape and name.

But when radioactivity destroys human cells and alters human genes, any living beings of the future would be no longer human but something grotesquely different. This scenario of the world's end is the most dreadful and sinister yet. What happened in Hiroshima twenty years ago was an absurdly horrendous massacre; but it may be the first harbinger of the world's real end, in which the human race as we know it will be succeeded by beings with blood and cells so ruined that they cannot be called human. The most terrifying monster lurking in the darkness of Hiroshima is precisely the possibility that man might become no longer human.

Five years ago when I visited Hiroshima for the first time, I wrote about how my heart shuddered as I looked at deformed specimens of *Veronica persica Poir* and chickenweed. Even now, the impression of the damage done to these lovely biennial plants, which grew in Hiroshima's irradiated soil, still haunts me. The original natural state of things, once damaged in this way, can never be fully recovered. If human blood and human cells are ever so damaged, it will be the beginning of the end of the human race. Accordingly, once we gain a proper perception of this possibility of humanity going out of existence, then it is no longer optional for us to be 'comrades of the A-bomb victims,' as Mr Kanai urges. Being their comrades becomes the only way we can remain true human beings. And if we would also be authentic human beings, then we already have impressive models in the Hiroshima people, such as Dr Shigeto, who have neither too little nor too much hope, who never surrender to any situation but courageously carry on with their day-to-day tasks.

# Notes

N.B. The notes were supplied by David L. Swain. The sole reference cited in the notes is *Hiroshima and Nagasaki: the Physical, Medical, and Social Effects of the Atomic Bombings* (New York: Basic Books Inc., Publishers, and Tokyo: Iwanami Shoten, Publishers, 1981), edited by the Committee for the Compilation of Materials on Damages Caused by the Atomic Bombs in Hiroshima and Nagasaki (Soichi Iijima, Seiji Imahori, Kanesaburo Gushima); translated from the Japanese by Eisei Ishikawa, M.D., and David L. Swain. This reference is abbreviated in the notes as *HN*.

1. The use of proceeds from New Year's postal card lotteries was among measures proposed for the relief of A-bomb victims. In September 1956 the Japanese Red Cross Society used such funds to found the Hiroshima A-bomb Hospital (120 beds) next to the Hiroshima Red Cross Hospital. *HN*, 546. The A-bomb Hospital now has 170 beds.

2. The leukocyte (white blood cell) count was related to the fear of leukemia. For technical discussion of leukemia among A-bomb victims, see *HN*, 238, 255-275; on early postbombing concern, see *HN*, 532-534.

3.   The first World Conference against Atomic and Hydrogen Bombs was held August 6-8, 1955, in Hiroshima.

4.   This simple phrase had a complicated history of domestic and international tension. By 1957 nuclear capabilities had escalated rapidly in number and power, as well as delivery systems. Peace movements throughout the world were becoming divided between those supporting liberation struggles in Asia and Africa and those favoring Western European-style opposition to nuclear weapons irrespective of political system — a rift that emerged in anti-nuclear world conferences from 1958 on. From 1960 anti-nuclear conferences also began to reflect the China-Soviet Union confrontation as well as, in Japan, a power struggle between Socialists and Communists. In 1964 the Japanese anti-nuclear movement split into the Japan Council against Atomic and Hydrogen Bombs (Gensuikyo) and the Japan Congress against Atomic and Hydrogen Bombs (Gensuikin). Immediate cause of the split was dispute over whether to oppose nuclear tests by 'any country,' capitalist or socialist, and over the value of the 1963 Limited Nuclear Test-ban Treaty. *HN*, 577-581.

5.   On March 1, 1954, the United States conducted a hydrogen bomb test on Bikini Atoll in the Marshall Islands in the Pacific Ocean. Radioactive fallout affected 239 inhabitants of three atolls in the area (of whom 46 died during the next twelve years); 28 American meterological observers; and 23 crewmen of the Japanese fishing vessel 'Lucky Dragon No 5,' one of whom died from radiation illness soon after the ship returned to its home port of Yaizu in Shizuoka Prefecture, Japan. *HN*, 4.

6.   A concrete arch over a granite stone marker close to the hypocenter of the atomic bomb's explosion, the Peace Memorial Cenotaph, like the Peace Memorial Park in which it stands, was designed by the Japanese architect, Kenzo Tange. *HN*, 604.

7.   '*Keloid* describes an overgrowth of scar tissue on the wound surface during the reparative process following thermal burn. . . . In this condition the tissue forms, on the skin surface, an

irregularly shaped protrusion which resembles the shell and legs of a crab.' *HN*, 191.

8.    Eba is a township (4.5 km from the hypocenter) in the southern part of Hiroshima City. Survivors fled in all directions from the central bombed area. *HN*, 356-357, 525; also figure 10.9.

9.    Some elderly survivors were fully orphaned, that is, they lost all family members. Others were quasi-orphaned; they had some surviving family member(s) but were forced, for some reason, to live apart in the same conditions as the fully orphaned. A 1960 survey showed that victims age seventy or over constituted 6.6 percent of Hiroshima's A-bomb victims. *HN*, 444.

10.    The Japan Communist Party had far fewer Diet members than the Japan Socialist Party (supported by the General Council of Trade Unions of Japan), but a stronger record of resisting the Pacific War. The JCP leaned toward China, the JSP toward Soviet Russia.

11.    The A-bomb Dome was formerly the Industrial Promotion Hall of Hiroshima Prefecture; it was designed by Jan Letzel, a Czech architect, and built in 1915 as one of Hiroshima's first modern buildings. Almost directly under the explosion point, the blast blew the roof in but exerted very little lateral pressure on the walls, which remained standing.

12.    The formal title of this organization is the Japan Confederation of A-bomb and H-bomb Suffers' Organizations; it consists of prefectural and local A-bomb victims' associations.

13.    The exposure of photographic film was one of the criteria used by Japan's leading atomic physicist, Yoshio Nishina, who was the first to confirm that the bombs dropped on Hiroshima and Nagasaki were atomic bombs. *HN*, 503-504.

14.    The Polaris submarine and the F-105D fighter plane were symbols of the U.S. Military presence in Japan.

15.    The A-bomb Victims Medical Care Law was passed on March 31, 1957; under this law, persons certified as having A-

bomb-caused medical problems are issued a passport-size health book and are eligible for various allowances and treatment. For classifications, benefits, and various revisions of this law, see *HN*, 547-551.

16.   The Otagawa River, which flows from north to south, fans out into seven branches (today, only six) that course through the delta center of Hiroshima City.

17.   Due to the schism in Japan's anti-nuclear movement that followed the Ninth World Conference (1963), a number of separate conferences were held in various cities in the summer of 1964. The three referred to here were the Tenth World Conference against A- and H-bombs held in Kyoto, sponsored by the Japan Council against A- and H-bombs, with Japan Communist Party support; and in Hiroshima, the International Conference (against A- and H-bombs), and the Three-Prefecture Liaison Conference, sponsored by the prefectures of Hiroshima, Nagasaki, and Shizuoka; both had the backing of the Japan Socialist Party and the General Council of Trade Unions of Japan (Sohyo). The Three-Prefecture Liaison (Sanken Rengo) later became the Japan Congress against A- and H-bombs.

18.   The International Conference was supported by the Japan Socialist Party and the General Council of Trade Unions of Japan (Sohyo).

19.   Sponsored by the Japan Council against A- and H-bombs, with the support of the Japan Communist Party.

20.   The August 1964 events in Hiroshima included, besides the major conferences, various meetings of A-bomb victims, academics, and other groups.

21.   During most of the ten-year period from the 1945 atomic bombings to the First World Conference in 1955, the Allied Occupation enforced silence on A-bomb matters (till 1951). Scholarly research picked up quickly after the occupation ended, but public discussion remained sparse until the 1954 Bikini test

sparked new interest that led to the First World Conference in 1955.

22.   Yaizu City in Shizuoka Prefecture was the home port of the fishing vessel 'Lucky Dragon No 5' which was showered with radioactive fallout from the 1954 hydrogen bomb test at Bikini Atoll. See n.5.

23.   At the time Mr Kanai spoke, no nationwide survey of A-bomb victims had been conducted by the national government; the first such survey (covering only A-bomb health-book holders) would be carried out as a supplement to the 1965 national census.

24.   A-bomb victims in Tokyo were estimated in the late 1970s at 10,000. The Tokyo metropolitan government from 1962 provided some support to the capital city's A-bomb victims supporters association, and later it initiated programs for victims, such as health examinations (1971), nursing allowances (1973), and health checkups for children of A-bomb victims (1974). This level of local government assistance to A-bomb victims is exceptional among Japan's cities other than Hiroshima and Nagasaki. *HN*, 562-563.

25.   'From enactment of the A-bomb Victims Medical Care Law in 1957 through 1964, the aggregate number of health checkups given in Hiroshima was 367,413; of these, 70,309 were given complete examinations.' *HN*, 545-546. These figures cover persons qualified for benefits under the law. *HN*, 547. Not until April 1965 was the law's scope broadened to provide 'health checkups for those desiring them.' *HN*, 549.

26.   The conference held in Kyoto represented the Japan Council-Japan Communist Party position. See n.17.

27.   The principal cause of disfigurations was keloid scars (see n.6), although in some cases there were other severe scar conditions. *HN*, 537-540.

28.   The Council for Investigation and Research into A-bomb Diseases in 1954 reported that 'many victims complained of

various vague and obscure subjective [ie felt by the victims but not discernible to doctors] symptoms. . . . The complaints of vague suffering without any characteristic disease should be regarded as one kind of chronic A-bomb illness. . . . Specific efficacious therapies for chronic A-bomb illness are not yet known. Indeed, if the main cause of illness is taken to be the after-effects of radiation injury, then there is no known therapy.' *HN*, 541.

29.  This explanation may have been a lay person's guess; but at least one medical specialist reported that drinking alcohol gave rapid relief from radiation symptoms. *HN*, 534.

30.  In moxa therapy, the powdered moxa is burned on the skin surface at one of the invisible (but histologically indistinguishable) sensitive points, traditionally 365 in number, that are also the loci of acupuncture therapy. This traditional therapy was introduced to Japan from China in the 7th century A.D.

31.  Nihon Hoso Kyokai (NHK, or Japan Broadcasting Corporation) is the sole non-commercial public corporation for broadcasting in Japan. Beginning radio broadcasts in 1925 and television broadcasts in 1953, its revenue depends on fees collected from receiving households, authorized by the 1950 Broadcast Law. Today, no charge is made for radio reception.

32.  The government of Japan did not adopt any official policy for aid to A-bomb victims until 1954, following the groundswell of public concern stirred by the Bikini H-bomb test. Subsequent national programs for care of A-bomb victims came almost always as responses to efforts by the victims, by nationwide peace movements, and by various Hiroshima- and Nagasaki-based organizations. *HN*, 552.

33.  Postal lottery proceeds also funded the Nagasaki A-bomb Hospital (81 beds; founded in 1958) and welfare centers for A-bomb victims in Nagasaki (1960) and Hiroshima (1961). The Hiroshima A-bomb Hospital from September 1956 to August 1965 had 210,954 outpatients and 2,248 inpatients, of whom 404 (17.9 percent) died. *HN*, 545, 546.

34.   The 1964 Olympic Games were held October 10-24 in Tokyo, Japan.

35.   The translation here is from the Japanese version by Sotokichi Kusaka.

36.   Louis-Ferdinand Céline (1894-1961), *Le Voyage au Bout de la Nuit.*

37.   *Hiroshima Genbaku Iryoshi,* 1961. Published by Hiroshima Genbaku Shogai Taisaku Kyogikai [Hiroshima A-bomb Casualty Council], Hiroshima.

38.   Malformed flowers of *Veronica persica Poir* are shown in Figure 5.5 of *HN* (p.85).

39.   Scientists from the Technology Agency, the Imperial Headquarters, the army and navy, Kyoto and Osaka imperial universities, and the Institute for Physical and Chemical Research in Tokyo entered Hiroshima and Nagasaki soon after the atomic bombings. At a joint army-navy meeting held August 10 under the auspices of the Imperial Headquarters, it was first confirmed that the bombs were atomic bombs. Various random measurements for radioactivity, however, indicated the need for systematic measurement, which was not begun until September 1945. *HN,* 503-504.

40.   On September 19, 1945, the Allied Occupation GHQ issued a press code restricting reference to A-bomb matters in speech, reporting, and publication. The GHQ's Economic and Scientific Bureau later announced that surveys and studies of A-bomb matters by the Japanese would require permission from GHQ, and publication of A-bomb data was prohibited. These restrictions remained in force until the occupation ended with the signing of the San Francisco Peace Treaty on September 8, 1951 (effective April 28, 1952). *HN,* 508, 620.

41.   Seiji Imahori, *Gensuibaku Jidai — Gendaishi no Shogen.* 2 vols. Tokyo: San'ichi shobo, 1959-1960.

42.   The primary effects of A-bomb illness and injury largely improved within four to six months after the bombings, but the

initial improvement proved deceptive. The first shock to people after the brief respite was the appearance of abnormal scar tissue (the notorious keloid) which, by the end of 1945, had become a serious problem; and, at this stage, surgically removed keloids tended to recur. Then, there was a marked increase in radiation symptoms in 1946. *HN*, 5, 537.

43.   The U.S. Army Surgeons Investigation Team was organized in early September 1945 by the GHQ Chief Surgeon; it collaborated with the Special Manhattan Engineer District Investigating Group in surveying the medical effects of the atomic bombings. (Japanese scientists were eventually included to form the Japan-U.S. Joint Commission for the Investigation of the Effects of the Atomic Bomb in Japan, and a survey report was completed in late December of 1945.) *HN*, 508-509.

44.   In its postwar economic recovery, Japan relied mainly on oil, which in the 1960s was still cheap; thus, coal mining areas were severely depressed.

45.   This discovery was a common factor in the psychological recovery of many A-bomb victims. *HN*, 490-491.

46.   Daughter of Marie (1867-1934) and Pierre (1859-1906) Curie, and wife of Frédéric Joliot-Curie (1900-1958), French physicist.

47.   See n.17.

48.   At the time, the Ryukyu Islands were still under U.S. administration; the agreement for their reversion to Japanese administration was signed June 17, 1971 (effective May 15, 1972).

49.   Privately published in Hiroshima, 1964.

50.   On July 11, 1966, the Hiroshima municipal assembly voted in favor of permanent preservation of the A-bomb Dome.

51.   These drawings of A-bomb scenes were exhibited throughout Japan from 1950; a 1953 exhibition in Nagasaki, for example, drew 17,500 viewers. *HN*, 574. The two artists later built an art gallery in Higashi Matsuyama, Saitama Prefecture (near Tokyo);

it includes their twelve mural-size 'Hiroshima Panels,' which in 1968 were exhibited in the United States.

52. *Pika-Don.* Tokyo: Potsdam Shoten, 1950. The 1979 revised edition of this small volume of A-bomb drawings has both Japanese and English captions (issued by Roba no Mimi group, Tokyo).

53. Immediately following the atomic explosion over Hiroshima, a huge 'mushroom cloud' hung over the city; half an hour later, conflagration broke out and a fire storm swept the city. At the peak of the fire (11 am-3 pm), a strong tornado developed toward the northern part of Hiroshima. Black clouds and smoke moved in a northwest direction, dropping the 'black rain' that carried radioactive fallout. This rain was actually black and also sticky. Fish died in rivers where it fell; diarrhea was experienced by cattle that ate grass contaminated by the murky rain. People adversely affected by the rain were known as secondary victims. A similar 'black rain' fell on Nagasaki, *HN*, 91-92, 357.

54. *Kojinteki na Taiken.* Tokyo: Shinchosha, 1964. Available in English under the title *A Personal Matter*, translated by John Nathan (New York: Grove Press Inc., 1968; Tokyo: Charles E. Tuttle Company, 1969).

55. The reference is to the *Ojo Yoshu* (A collection of essentials concerning rebirth in the Western Paradise), written in 984-985 by the Buddhist priest Genshin (942-1017) of the Tendai sect; this work had a major influence in the founding of the Pure Land (Jodo) and True Pure Land (Jodo Shin) sects. Emperor Enyu (reigned 969-984) commissioned the painting, based on this work, of the 'ten levels of the universe,' including graphic depiction of karmic retribution in hell (*jigoku*).